JUMBLE® CROSSWORDS™ Jamboree

A Puzzle Party for All Ages

David L. Hoyt

TRIUMPH BOOKS
CHICAGO

This book is available in quantity at special discounts
for your group or organization.
For further information, contact:

Triumph Books
542 South Dearborn Street
Suite 750
Chicago, Illinois 60605
(312) 939-3330
Fax (312) 663-3557

Printed in U.S.A.

ISBN-13: 978-1-57243-787-6
ISBN-10: 1-57243-787-1

Contents

JUMBLE CROSSWORDS® Jamboree™

CHAMPION

PUZZLES

JUMBLE® CROSSWORDS™

ACROSS

CLUE	ANSWER
1. Trite expression	HEICLC
5. ______ chicken	DIREF
6. ______ Coast	YRIOV
7. Scheduled	TSDEAL

DOWN

CLUE	ANSWER
1. Oblong box	FCNIFO
2. First	NITILIA
3. Lair	DHOETIU
4. Competed in a sport	AYEPDL

CLUE: The size of the first ____ on the moon was about 13 inches long.

BONUS ○○○○○○○○○

How to play: Complete the crossword puzzle by looking at the clues and unscrambling the answers. When the puzzle is complete, unscramble the circled letters to solve the BONUS.

JUMBLE® CROSSWORDS™

ACROSS

CLUE	ANSWER
1. Confusion	EAMMHY
5. Australian city	TRPEH
6. Type of scarf	ATOCS
7. Abundance	TLAHEW

DOWN

CLUE	ANSWER
1. Sugar ______	PMELSA
2. Length	ADGREAY
3. Moral	LTEAHIC
4. Comedy ______	HKSTCE

CLUE: Early Spanish sailors called this site *Cayo Hueso* (Bone Island).

BONUS 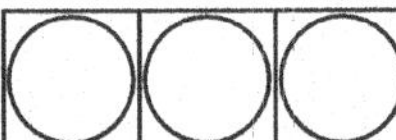 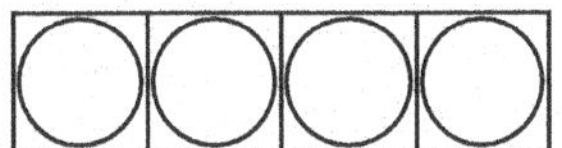

How to play: Complete the crossword puzzle by looking at the clues and unscrambling the answers. When the puzzle is complete, unscramble the circled letters to solve the BONUS.

ACROSS

CLUE	ANSWER
1. ______ plant	MTTAOO
5. Republic of ______	HNAAG
6. To guide a person	UHRES
7. Bird ______	DEEERF

DOWN

CLUE	ANSWER
1. Powerful animals	RISTEG
2. Determine	AEEMUSR
3. Vandalized	HRATSDE
4. Point maker	RCSREO

CLUE: A daily occurrence

BONUS

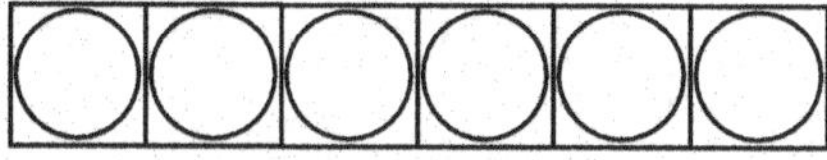

How to play: Complete the crossword puzzle by looking at the clues and unscrambling the answers. When the puzzle is complete, unscramble the circled letters to solve the BONUS.

ACROSS

CLUE	ANSWER
1. Snagged	UACHTG
5. Green ______	HMUTB
6. Undo, loosen	ENUIT
7. Armor-______	DPTAEL

DOWN

CLUE	ANSWER
1. Cows	ATETLC
2. Infrequent	LSNAUUU
3. Natural ______	AIBTAHT
4. Circulate, broadcast	PSERDA

CLUE: This invention dates back thousands of years.

BONUS 

How to play: Complete the crossword puzzle by looking at the clues and unscrambling the answers. When the puzzle is complete, unscramble the circled letters to solve the BONUS.

JUMBLE® CROSSWORDS™

ACROSS

CLUE	ANSWER
1. English scientist	NNOETW
5. Supports	PSROP
6. Prize	ERUPS
7. Pressing	TRNGUE

DOWN

CLUE	ANSWER
1. Incendiary mixture	LPANMA
2. Lie	RPOPHEW
3. See	BVSOREE
4. Duplicity	DCTEIE

CLUE: This place is home to nearly eight hundred thousand people.

BONUS 

How to play: Complete the crossword puzzle by looking at the clues and unscrambling the answers. When the puzzle is complete, unscramble the circled letters to solve the BONUS.

JUMBLE® CROSSWORDS™

ACROSS

CLUE	ANSWER
1. Indeed	LAERYL
5. Type of beverage	RAEGL
6. Relative magnitudes	TIRAO
7. Front	DACAEF

DOWN

CLUE	ANSWER
1. Decision	LGURIN
2. Home to Biskra	RAAILEG
3. ______ Young	TERALOT
4. Grow to be	EOEMBC

CLUE: Type of turn

BONUS

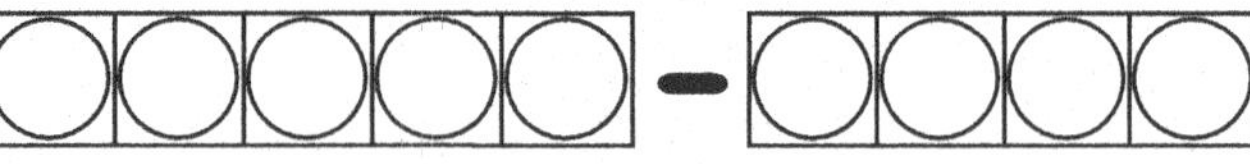

How to play

Complete the crossword puzzle by looking at the clues and unscrambling the answers. When the puzzle is complete, unscramble the circled letters to solve the BONUS.

JUMBLE® CROSSWORDS™

ACROSS

CLUE	ANSWER
1. Made well again	LDHAEE
5. Subside	EPASL
6. ______ peace	NIREN
7. Type of carbohydrate	TCRAHS

DOWN

CLUE	ANSWER
1. Assistant	PRLEHE
2. Name	TIANPOP
3. FDR's wife	LOEAERN
4. ______ party	ECSRAH

CLUE: Ineffective

BONUS 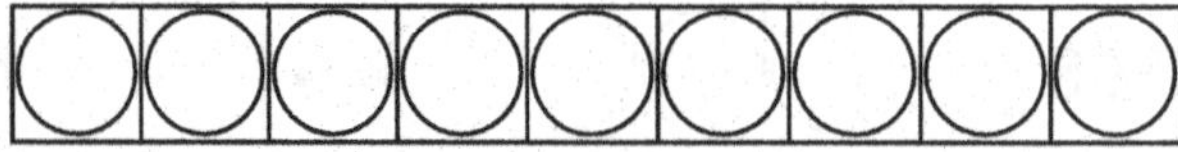

How to play: Complete the crossword puzzle by looking at the clues and unscrambling the answers. When the puzzle is complete, unscramble the circled letters to solve the BONUS.

JUMBLE® CROSSWORDS™

ACROSS

CLUE	ANSWER
1. Beginner	NECOIV
5. Sweet ______	LBIAS
6. Lure	PETTM
7. Type of bird	ERLOIO

DOWN

CLUE	ANSWER
1. Caught	ANDEBB
2. Guest	RVIOSIT
3. P.F. role	MLBOUCO
4. Tea ______	TEELTK

CLUE: This actor was the youngest student ever accepted into Juilliard's drama department.

BONUS 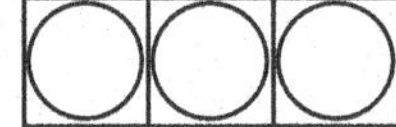 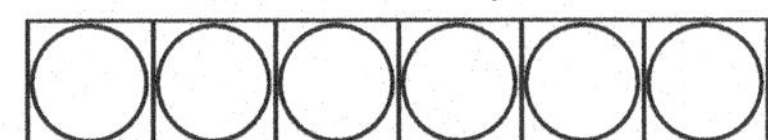

How to play: Complete the crossword puzzle by looking at the clues and unscrambling the answers. When the puzzle is complete, unscramble the circled letters to solve the BONUS.

JUMBLE® CROSSWORDS™

ACROSS

CLUE	ANSWER
1. Thief	BRREBO
5. ______ game	HLELS
6. Motivate	PMILE
7. Menace	RHTAET

DOWN

CLUE	ANSWER
1. Roll	EORRTS
2. Flaw	HLBMEIS
3. Solar ______	PLEIECS
4. Mold	UPCSTL

CLUE: Value

BONUS 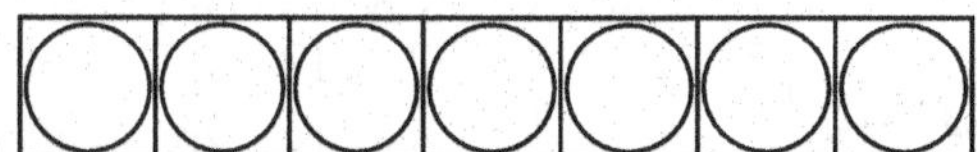

How to play Complete the crossword puzzle by looking at the clues and unscrambling the answers. When the puzzle is complete, unscramble the circled letters to solve the BONUS.

ACROSS

CLUE	ANSWER
1. A U.S. city	WENKRA
5. Craze	NAAIM
6. Al or Jerry	EISLW
7. Worn	ARYEFD

DOWN

CLUE	ANSWER
1. Positive ______	URMNEB
2. Henry ______	NKRIWLE
3. Street	AWORDYA
4. Threw	EOSDTS

CLUE: This man said, "Everyone is a moon, and has a dark side which he never shows to anybody."

BONUS 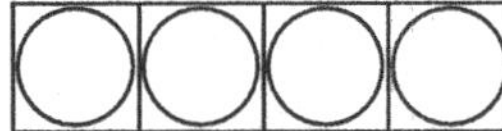 

How to play: Complete the crossword puzzle by looking at the clues and unscrambling the answers. When the puzzle is complete, unscramble the circled letters to solve the BONUS.

JUMBLE® CROSSWORDS™

ACROSS

CLUE	ANSWER
1. Spurn	ETJREC
5. Tailed orbiter	MOCTE
6. The ______ Sea	RISIH
7. Struck	EAHBDS

DOWN

CLUE	ANSWER
1. Recover	UEPROC
2. ______ Bay	AMICJAA
3. Type of fish	TASCIFH
4. Whipped	HLDEAS

CLUE: Repeat

BONUS 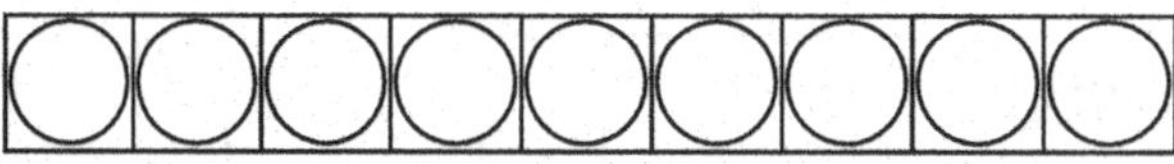

How to play: Complete the crossword puzzle by looking at the clues and unscrambling the answers. When the puzzle is complete, unscramble the circled letters to solve the BONUS.

JUMBLE® CROSSWORDS™

ACROSS

CLUE	ANSWER
1. Apex	NHEIZT
5. ______ Baker	ANAIT
6. Significant ______	HRTOE
7. Type of insect	AADICC

DOWN

CLUE	ANSWER
1. Fanatic	AZTOLE
2. African city	RAINOIB
3. Type of passageway	TRCAHAE
4. ______ Nevada	RIAESR

CLUE: This top-rated TV show filmed 430 episodes.

BONUS 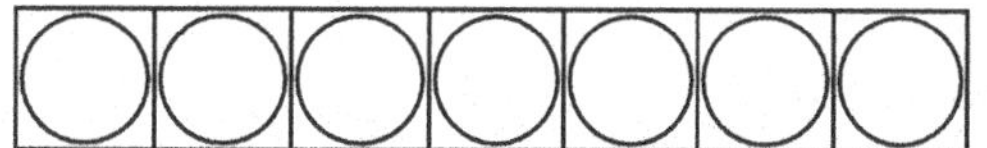

How to play: Complete the crossword puzzle by looking at the clues and unscrambling the answers. When the puzzle is complete, unscramble the circled letters to solve the BONUS.

JUMBLE® CROSSWORDS™

ACROSS

CLUE	ANSWER
1. Last _____	EDCOSN
5. Edge	TIMLI
6. Fossil resin	BRMEA
7. European city	EANVEG

DOWN

CLUE	ANSWER
1. A Tom Hanks movie	HPLSAS
2. Equate	MCRAOEP
3. Memorable	NTLEBAO
4. _____ Mist	ARSERI

CLUE: In 1913 a wooden bridge was built from the mainland to this.

BONUS 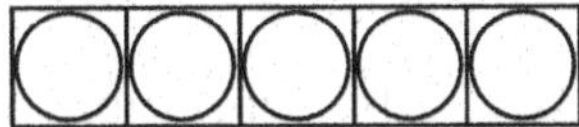 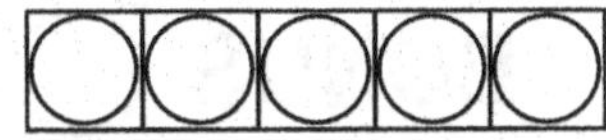

How to play: Complete the crossword puzzle by looking at the clues and unscrambling the answers. When the puzzle is complete, unscramble the circled letters to solve the BONUS.

JUMBLE® CROSSWORDS™

ACROSS

CLUE	ANSWER
1. Counter	CUBASA
5. ______ light	TILPO
6. Pay	EGAWS
7. Copy ______	RDTIOE

DOWN

CLUE	ANSWER
1. Angle	CSAPTE
2. Permitted	ALDOELW
3. Tense	TIUHPGT
4. Pointer	RUSCRO

CLUE: A type of prediction

BONUS 

How to play: Complete the crossword puzzle by looking at the clues and unscrambling the answers. When the puzzle is complete, unscramble the circled letters to solve the BONUS.

JUMBLE® CROSSWORDS™

ACROSS

CLUE	ANSWER
1. Just _____	RYELBA
5. Lookout	IAVTS
6. A U.S. city	AAMHO
7. Stick	EAREHD

DOWN

CLUE	ANSWER
1. Bison, for example	NBEOIV
2. Answer	PNOSRED
3. Unwanted discharge	AELGKAE
4. Adorned	TNROEA

CLUE: The first of its kind was published in 1878.

BONUS

How to play: Complete the crossword puzzle by looking at the clues and unscrambling the answers. When the puzzle is complete, unscramble the circled letters to solve the BONUS.

JUMBLE® CROSSWORDS™

ACROSS

CLUE	ANSWER
1. Cushion	RFFEUB
5. Type of restaurant	ERIDN
6. Wet	YGGSO
7. Required	DDEEEN

DOWN

CLUE	ANSWER
1. Harass	DRBEGA
2. Skillful handling	EFSISNE
3. Angered	EDENGRA
4. Influenced	WEYADS

CLUE: The _____ _____ is 1,885 miles long.

BONUS 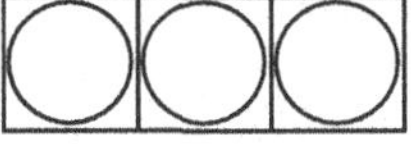 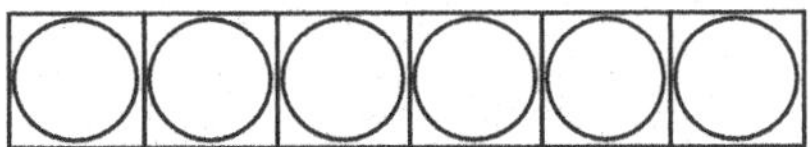

How to play: Complete the crossword puzzle by looking at the clues and unscrambling the answers. When the puzzle is complete, unscramble the circled letters to solve the BONUS.

JUMBLE® CROSSWORDS™

ACROSS

CLUE	ANSWER
1. ______ oil	RSAOTC
5. Lower animal	SETAB
6. Lowness of spirits	LOMOG
7. Bind	ERDHAE

DOWN

CLUE	ANSWER
1. A magnetic metal	LBAOCT
2. Caught	DSGNEGA
3. Beaten	NUDOTEO
4. Hinder	YIMETS

CLUE: This word first appeared on maps in the 1500s.

BONUS 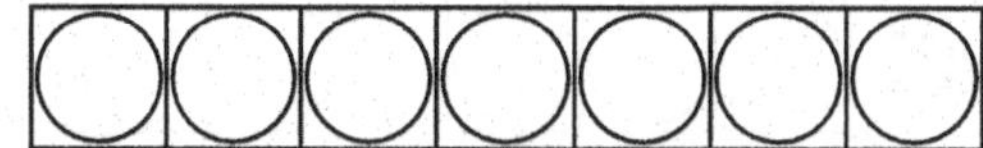

How to play: Complete the crossword puzzle by looking at the clues and unscrambling the answers. When the puzzle is complete, unscramble the circled letters to solve the BONUS.

JUMBLE® CROSSWORDS™

ACROSS

CLUE	ANSWER
1. Witty comedy	RTIASE
5. Move quickly	OTOCS
6. ______ name	DRNAB
7. Precious stones	LWESJE

DOWN

CLUE	ANSWER
1. Buddy ______	YTMSES
2. Drawback	BTOLURE
3. Go over again	ERCRAET
4. Mass ______	DUXOSE

CLUE: This place is called the "Land of Enchantment."

BONUS  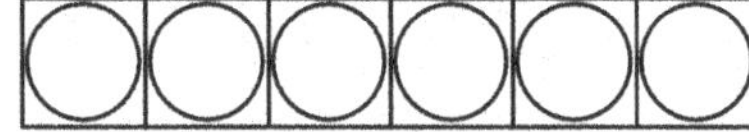

How to play: Complete the crossword puzzle by looking at the clues and unscrambling the answers. When the puzzle is complete, unscramble the circled letters to solve the BONUS.

JUMBLE® CROSSWORDS™

ACROSS

CLUE	ANSWER
1. Cursed	MNDDEA
5. Ravine	LCUGH
6. Flowing garments	RESBO
7. Christmas _____	TAUCCS

DOWN

CLUE	ANSWER
1. Absorb	TISDEG
2. Type of disease	ALIARMA
3. Show	XITIBEH
4. Banquets	SFATES

CLUE: A mountain range, with peaks more than twelve thousand feet high, runs through this country from northwest to southeast.

BONUS 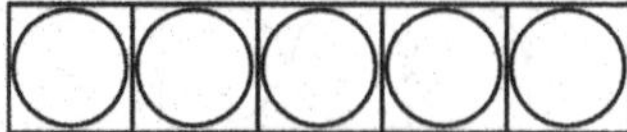 

How to play — Complete the crossword puzzle by looking at the clues and unscrambling the answers. When the puzzle is complete, unscramble the circled letters to solve the BONUS.

JUMBLE® CROSSWORDS™

ACROSS

CLUE	ANSWER
1. A third sign	NIEMIG
5. Definable aspect	AETCF
6. Jeremy _____	RISNO
7. Undermine	AKNEEW

DOWN

CLUE	ANSWER
1. Talented	DTIFEG
2. _____ shop	HANMEIC
3. Television _____	KTENOWR
4. A life _____	ESONLS

CLUE: This U.S. state capital lies on an isthmus between lakes Monona and Mendota.

BONUS 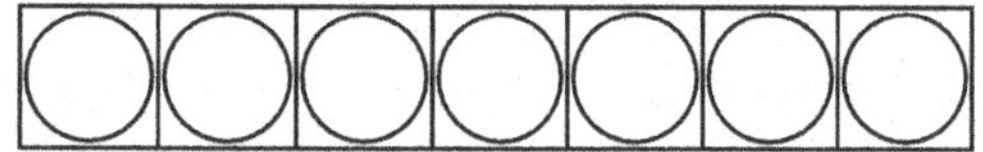

How to play: Complete the crossword puzzle by looking at the clues and unscrambling the answers. When the puzzle is complete, unscramble the circled letters to solve the BONUS.

JUMBLE® CROSSWORDS™

CLUE	ACROSS	ANSWER
1. Chopped		DNMEIC
5. Group		PULCM
6. ______ number		TOERU
7. Shirt part		ELVESE

CLUE	DOWN	ANSWER
1. Ridiculed		KMCDEO
2. Indifferent		LEUNRTA
3. Advocate		PSEUOES
4. Blue ______		HESECE

CLUE: This actor turned down the lead role in *Jerry Maguire*.

BONUS 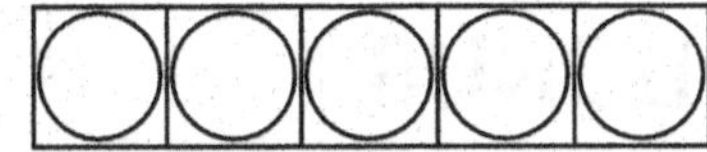

How to play: Complete the crossword puzzle by looking at the clues and unscrambling the answers. When the puzzle is complete, unscramble the circled letters to solve the BONUS.

JUMBLE® CROSSWORDS™

ACROSS

CLUE	ANSWER
1. Develop	VEVELO
5. Flawless	AEDIL
6. Tent post	TEKSA
7. Aristocracy	NTREYG

DOWN

CLUE	ANSWER
1. Left	XDEEIT
2. Manage	SRVEEOE
3. Brave	LAVAITN
4. Fix	MERDEY

CLUE: This product hit store shelves in the midtwenties.

BONUS

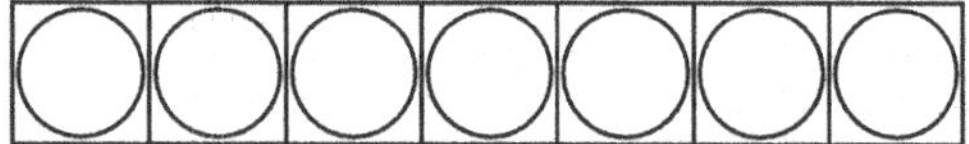

How to play: Complete the crossword puzzle by looking at the clues and unscrambling the answers. When the puzzle is complete, unscramble the circled letters to solve the BONUS.

JUMBLE® CROSSWORDS™

ACROSS

CLUE	**ANSWER**
1. Club or gun	NEWOPA
5. Digestive ______	ATTRC
6. Rise quickly	PSKEI
7. Arrival	ENTDAV

DOWN

CLUE	**ANSWER**
1. Swampy	RTWYEA
2. Assembled	ASAEDMS
3. Silhouette	TOILUEN
4. Introduce forcefully	JNECIT

CLUE: At age 10, this actor sent his résumé to *The Carol Burnett Show.*

BONUS  

How to play Complete the crossword puzzle by looking at the clues and unscrambling the answers. When the puzzle is complete, unscramble the circled letters to solve the BONUS.

JUMBLE® CROSSWORDS™

ACROSS

CLUE	ANSWER
1. Best _____	DFIRNE
5. Loathe	BOHRA
6. Pile	DNUMO
7. _____ a shot	NCEJIT

DOWN

CLUE	ANSWER
1. Flamboyant	LYASFH
2. Barbarous	HNIMUNA
3. Foster	UENRTUR
4. Outlaw	DBNAIT

CLUE: This woman said, "I'm too tall to be a girl, I never had enough dresses to be a lady, I wouldn't call myself a woman. I'd say I'm somewhere between a chick and a broad."

BONUS ○○○○○ ○○○○○○○

How to play: Complete the crossword puzzle by looking at the clues and unscrambling the answers. When the puzzle is complete, unscramble the circled letters to solve the BONUS.

JUMBLE CROSSWORDS™

ACROSS

CLUE	ANSWER
1. Moon motions	BROIST
5. Faux pas	ROERR
6. TV sitcom from 1976 to 1985	ECIAL
7. Open	WNPARU

DOWN

CLUE	ANSWER
1. Premiere	RPOENE
2. Deal	ANBIRGA
3. Canine breed	RREITER
4. Composition	KAUEPM

CLUE: ______, ______, is home to approximately 7 million people. It was called the "City of Kings" when it was founded in the 1500s.

BONUS 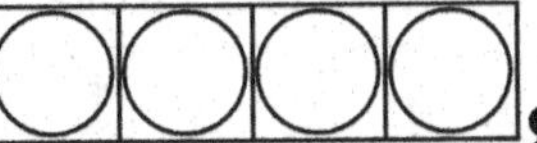 , 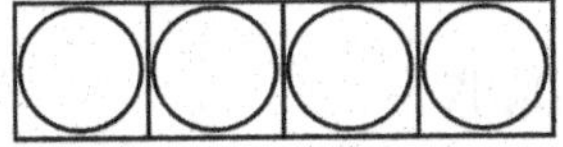

How to play: Complete the crossword puzzle by looking at the clues and unscrambling the answers. When the puzzle is complete, unscramble the circled letters to solve the BONUS.

ACROSS

CLUE	ANSWER
1. ______ fuel	ELSEID
5. ______ hand	PERPU
6. Bet	RGAWE
7. ______ shower	DIRBLA

DOWN

CLUE	ANSWER
1. Twofold	LUEOBD
2. Enable	MREPEWO
3. Angered	DERENGA
4. Security unit	ALOTPR

CLUE: This city, which is home to about eight hundred thousand people, was the site of the first umbrella factory in the United States.

BONUS 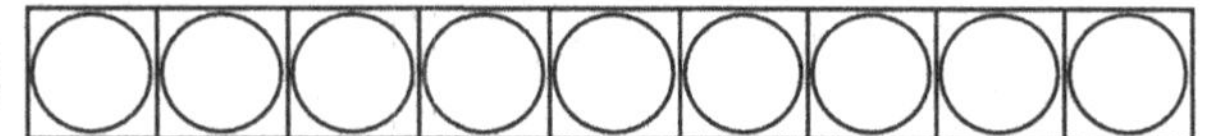

How to play: Complete the crossword puzzle by looking at the clues and unscrambling the answers. When the puzzle is complete, unscramble the circled letters to solve the BONUS.

JUMBLE® CROSSWORDS™

ACROSS

CLUE	ANSWER
1. Memorable	AHCYTC
5. Remains	NSIRU
6. Best	TLEIE
7. Aquatic mammals	ETSOTR

DOWN

CLUE	ANSWER
1. Cerebral ______	ROCXTE
2. Three-pronged spear	TIREDTN
3. Unfriendly	EISTHOL
4. Water-______	KSEISR

CLUE: The first U.S. ______ was authorized on March 1, 1790.

BONUS 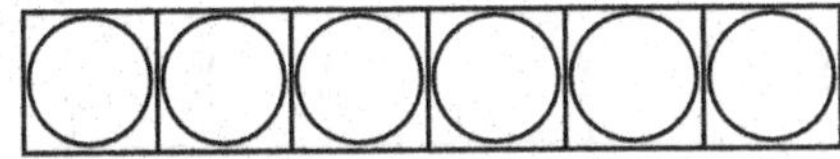

How to play: Complete the crossword puzzle by looking at the clues and unscrambling the answers. When the puzzle is complete, unscramble the circled letters to solve the BONUS.

JUMBLE® CROSSWORDS™

ACROSS

CLUE	ANSWER
1. Downhearted	LOFEWU
5. Soft, smooth	YSKIL
6. Angel-hair ______	TPSAA
7. Spring	ESRYGE

DOWN

CLUE	ANSWER
1. Knowledge	MDIOSW
2. Oval	LLIEESP
3. Odysseus	YSSELSU
4. Silky goat hair	HRIOAM

CLUE: The ______, which was not much larger than a modern tennis court, held about 100 people.

BONUS 

How to play: Complete the crossword puzzle by looking at the clues and unscrambling the answers. When the puzzle is complete, unscramble the circled letters to solve the BONUS.

JUMBLE® CROSSWORDS™

CLUE	ACROSS	ANSWER
1. Type of hat		DEFROA
5. City in Iraq		AARSB
6. Speak		ETUTR
7. Closer		RREEAN

CLUE	DOWN	ANSWER
1. Fifties heartthrob		BIAFAN
2. Conflict		DEITUSP
3. Cooker		RAROTSE
4. Carrier, holder		AERREB

CLUE: Until 1796, this state was called Franklin.

BONUS 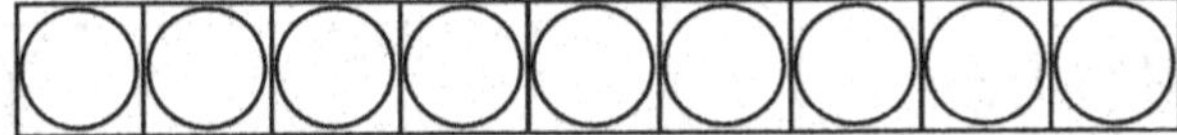

How to play: Complete the crossword puzzle by looking at the clues and unscrambling the answers. When the puzzle is complete, unscramble the circled letters to solve the BONUS.

ACROSS

CLUE	ANSWER
1. Extra	XESSCE
5. Ice ______	TWARE
6. Drop ______	NOZSE
7. Reverse	NRTIEV

DOWN

CLUE	ANSWER
1. ______ Norton	DWADRE
2. Inhabitant	NTEICIZ
3. Unfamiliar	RTSNAEG
4. Water ______	LECSOT

CLUE: The first prisoners arrived at ______ on August 11, 1934.

BONUS

How to play: Complete the crossword puzzle by looking at the clues and unscrambling the answers. When the puzzle is complete, unscramble the circled letters to solve the BONUS.

ACROSS

CLUE	ANSWER
1. Contraption	TGGEAD
5. ______ script	EOMIV
6. Rent	AELES
7. Sitcom uncle	FREETS

DOWN

CLUE	ANSWER
1. Calculated move	MGTBIA
2. Tell	EUDIGLV
3. Stately	LEETNAG
4. ______ shower	RTMEEO

CLUE: The first major league baseball game ever played ______ was played on April 12, 1965.

BONUS 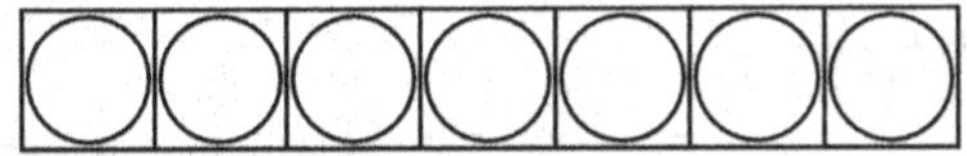

How to play: Complete the crossword puzzle by looking at the clues and unscrambling the answers. When the puzzle is complete, unscramble the circled letters to solve the BONUS.

JUMBLE® CROSSWORDS™

ACROSS

CLUE	ANSWER
1. The ______ Islands	MCYNAA
5. Move forward steadily	RFEOG
6. Performer	TCARO
7. Gregor Johann ______	NMLEED

DOWN

CLUE	ANSWER
1. ______ corner	FCNIFO
2. Distance	ERGYAAD
3. Avoided	ADEVTRE
4. ______ car	TPLORA

CLUE: In 1888, this was the first European country to establish a system for health insurance for its workers.

BONUS 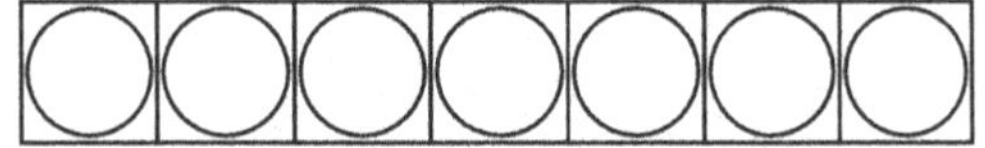

How to play: Complete the crossword puzzle by looking at the clues and unscrambling the answers. When the puzzle is complete, unscramble the circled letters to solve the BONUS.

JUMBLE® CROSSWORDS™

ACROSS

CLUE	ANSWER
1. Power	LSCEMU
5. Type of bird	NREAV
6. White _____	EIONS
7. Nappy	HGAGSY

DOWN

CLUE	ANSWER
1. Large fish	NMIALR
2. Saturday or July	HEVESNT
3. Touchdown	NALGIND
4. Extensively	LIEDYW

CLUE: _____, _____, has more homeless cats per square mile than any other city in the world.

BONUS ◯◯◯◯, ◯◯◯◯◯

How to play: Complete the crossword puzzle by looking at the clues and unscrambling the answers. When the puzzle is complete, unscramble the circled letters to solve the BONUS.

JUMBLE® CROSSWORDS™

CLUE **ACROSS** **ANSWER**

1. Third-______ burn — R E G E D E
5. First-______ — A L S C S
6. Type of structure — L O G I O
7. Table ______ — N T E S I N

CLUE **DOWN** **ANSWER**

1. Agenda — D C T O E K
2. Hard rock — R A G I N E T
3. The fifth of its kind — P S E L I N O
4. Wading birds — N R E H O S

CLUE: This animal can weigh up to 300 pounds.

BONUS

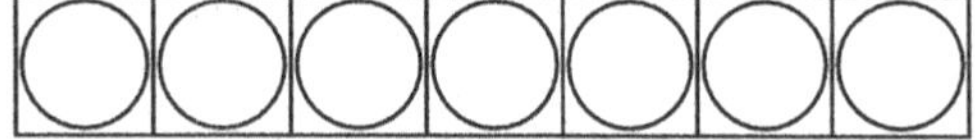

How to play — Complete the crossword puzzle by looking at the clues and unscrambling the answers. When the puzzle is complete, unscramble the circled letters to solve the BONUS.

JUMBLE® CROSSWORDS™

ACROSS

CLUE	ANSWER
1. A car or cat	AGARJU
5. Individual entity	HITNG
6. Arterial trunk	TRAAO
7. A time period	ECEDDA

DOWN

CLUE	ANSWER
1. George ______	TNEOJS
2. Type of look	REIGAMC
3. Bordered by Libya	LGIAREA
4. Perilous	NSUEAF

CLUE: This city is home to San José Church (founded c.1523), the oldest church in continuous use in the Western Hemisphere.

BONUS 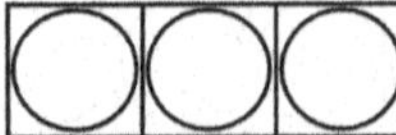 

How to play: Complete the crossword puzzle by looking at the clues and unscrambling the answers. When the puzzle is complete, unscramble the circled letters to solve the BONUS.

JUMBLE® CROSSWORDS™

ACROSS

CLUE	ANSWER
1. Bad	NREOTT
5. Direct	ETRSE
6. Home to Augusta	NAIEM
7. Precarious situation	HILTPG

DOWN

CLUE	ANSWER
1. Home to Arkhangelsk	USIARS
2. British ______ unit	HETMRLA
3. ______ power	RAEINGN
4. Customer	LCETIN

CLUE: This was Mrs. Howell's seldom-talked-about first name on *Gilligan's Island.*

BONUS 

How to play: Complete the crossword puzzle by looking at the clues and unscrambling the answers. When the puzzle is complete, unscramble the circled letters to solve the BONUS.

JUMBLE® CROSSWORDS™

ACROSS

CLUE	ANSWER
1. Each	PCEAIE
5. Grounds	AIBSS
6. Order	DCEIT
7. Smell	NTSHEC

DOWN

CLUE	ANSWER
1. Surprise	BMHUAS
2. Check out	NCTIEPS
3. Pin ______	USONCIH
4. 1985 C.C. movie	LCHFTE

CLUE: Alexander ______ was born in Nevis, British West Indies, in 1757.

BONUS 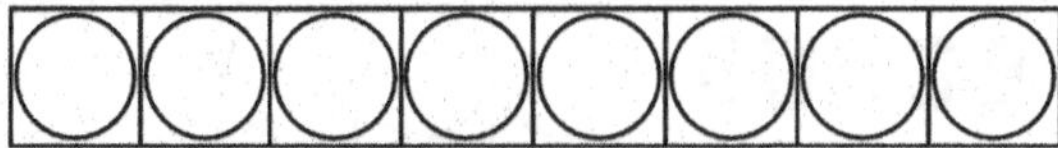

How to play: Complete the crossword puzzle by looking at the clues and unscrambling the answers. When the puzzle is complete, unscramble the circled letters to solve the BONUS.

JUMBLE® CROSSWORDS™

ACROSS

CLUE	ANSWER
1. Find	LETACO
5. ______ point	RAETX
6. Expeditiousness	HETAS
7. Boxes	TRCSEA

DOWN

CLUE	ANSWER
1. Room	ELWEYA
2. Type of receiver	RATCCEH
3. ______ system	TRITSNA
4. Casters	RTOVES

CLUE: This company, which is now part of a larger company, was founded in 1911.

BONUS 

How to play: Complete the crossword puzzle by looking at the clues and unscrambling the answers. When the puzzle is complete, unscramble the circled letters to solve the BONUS.

ACROSS

CLUE	ANSWER
1. Left quickly	TBLODE
5. Long-______	NAREG
6. Bert's bud	RNIEE
7. Chain ______	EROSST

DOWN

CLUE	ANSWER
1. ______ grounds	RIBLUA
2. Tolerant	NNELIET
3. ______ Rigby	REOLNAE
4. ______, Georgia	HTASNE

CLUE: Anastasia Island, Florida, was the site of the first ______ farm in the United States, established in 1892.

BONUS

How to play: Complete the crossword puzzle by looking at the clues and unscrambling the answers. When the puzzle is complete, unscramble the circled letters to solve the BONUS.

JUMBLE® CROSSWORDS™

ACROSS

CLUE	ANSWER
1. Struggle	ETFIRS
5. With	NOAMG
6. Perfectly suited	LIADE
7. Pens	EWSTRI

DOWN

CLUE	ANSWER
1. Pants	SKSLCA
2. More spacious	RMREOIO
3. Contrived idea	TFGNIEM
4. Fashions	ETSSLY

CLUE: It can take 10 minutes for a ______ to fall to Earth from one thousand feet.

BONUS 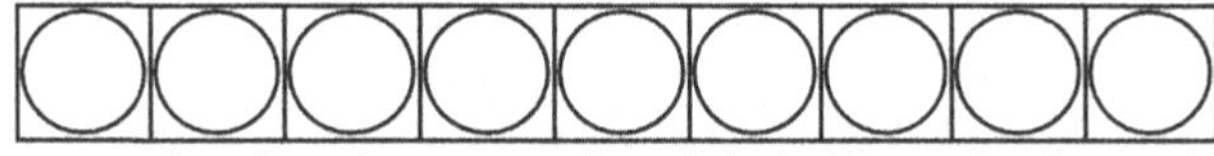

How to play: Complete the crossword puzzle by looking at the clues and unscrambling the answers. When the puzzle is complete, unscramble the circled letters to solve the BONUS.

JUMBLE® CROSSWORDS™

ACROSS

CLUE	ANSWER
1. Fierce	VESGAA
5. ______-class	RLWOD
6. Perfect	LIDAE
7. Dull	TOSYGD

DOWN

CLUE	ANSWER
1. Waste	WESEAG
2. Decision	RVCEIDT
3. Good fortune	DDOGESN
4. Potpourri	LEDMYE

CLUE: The ringgit is the official currency of this country

BONUS 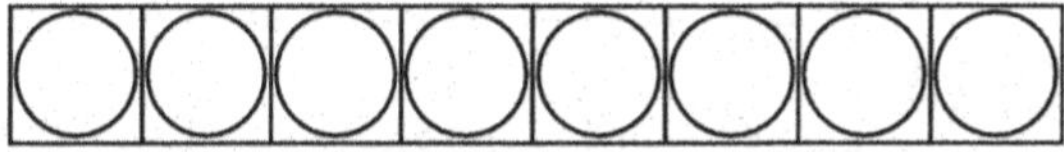

How to play: Complete the crossword puzzle by looking at the clues and unscrambling the answers. When the puzzle is complete, unscramble the circled letters to solve the BONUS.

JUMBLE® CROSSWORDS™

ACROSS

CLUE	ANSWER
1. Mel Gibson movie	NRMOSA
5. ______ year	HITGL
6. Christopher ______	EEREV
7. Type of song	BLDLAA

DOWN

CLUE	ANSWER
1. Yield	NERLET
2. Neighbor to Chad	AINREIG
3. Type of porridge	LTOEAAM
4. Story	NGEEDL

CLUE: On September 20, 1519, this man set sail with five ships and about 250 men.

BONUS 

How to play: Complete the crossword puzzle by looking at the clues and unscrambling the answers. When the puzzle is complete, unscramble the circled letters to solve the BONUS.

JUMBLE® CROSSWORDS™

ACROSS

CLUE	ANSWER
1. Empty	TAANCV
5. Former	RRPIO
6. Stop	BAEAT
7. Successful director	DHROAW

DOWN

CLUE	ANSWER
1. Fumes	PRASVO
2. Award-winning movie	AGHOICC
3. Ideal condition	RINAVAN
4. Protect	DDENFE

CLUE: Virtually certain

BONUS 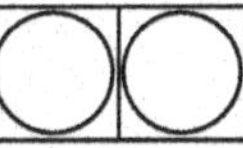 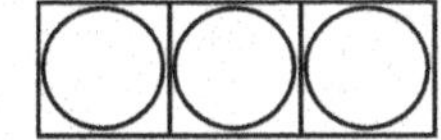 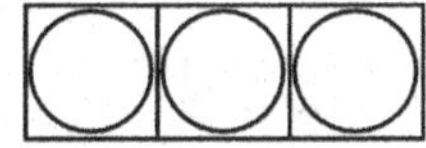

How to play: Complete the crossword puzzle by looking at the clues and unscrambling the answers. When the puzzle is complete, unscramble the circled letters to solve the BONUS.

JUMBLE® CROSSWORDS™

ACROSS

CLUE	ANSWER
1. ______ lizard	NUOLEG
5. Bone ______	HNIAC
6. Urge	MILPE
7. ______ weather	RSEEEV

DOWN

CLUE	ANSWER
1. Vicinity	AOLELC
2. Employ	ZTIUILE
3. Maintain a hold on	PRGLPAE
4. Put on ice	HVSEEL

CLUE: Large

BONUS 

How to play: Complete the crossword puzzle by looking at the clues and unscrambling the answers. When the puzzle is complete, unscramble the circled letters to solve the BONUS.

ACROSS

CLUE	ANSWER
1. Discuss again	HEHARS
5. Long-necked mammal	AMCLE
6. Annual award	ROACS
7. Polecats	KKSNUS

DOWN

CLUE	ANSWER
1. Withdraw	TERACN
2. Type of evergreen	MCEHOLK
3. ______ Valley	LISCINO
4. Spins	RLWSIT

CLUE: This show aired in the same time slot, Thursdays at 8:00 P.M. EST, during its entire nine-year run.

BONUS 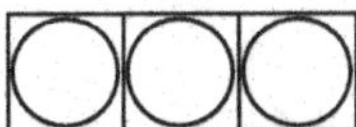 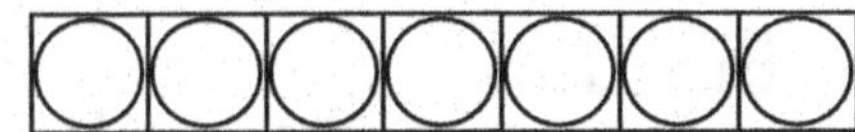

How to play: Complete the crossword puzzle by looking at the clues and unscrambling the answers. When the puzzle is complete, unscramble the circled letters to solve the BONUS.

ACROSS

CLUE	ANSWER
1. A marine decapod	MIRPSH
5. Unsettle	PTUSE
6. Type of candy	DFEGU
7. Proclaims loudly	RALEBS

DOWN

CLUE	ANSWER
1. Snubs	UPSNRS
2. Relaxing	EULRTFS
3. Type of fighter	ATMAROD
4. Gliders	KRSSIE

CLUE: Frame

BONUS

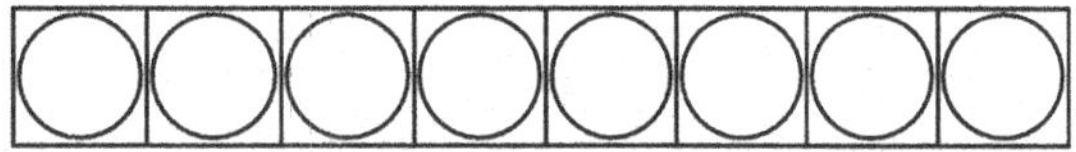

How to play: Complete the crossword puzzle by looking at the clues and unscrambling the answers. When the puzzle is complete, unscramble the circled letters to solve the BONUS.

JUMBLE® CROSSWORDS™

CLUE	ACROSS	ANSWER
1. ______ out		UGIEFR
5. Metallic sound		NLGCA
6. English actor		RISNO
7. Gun or sword		AOEWNP

CLUE	DOWN	ANSWER
1. Fear ______		RCAOFT
2. "The ______ State"		ARTGINE
3. Reorganize		PRRGEOU
4. Moyet or Krauss		NLOISA

CLUE: _____ _____ measures about 175 feet from top to bottom.

BONUS ◯◯◯◯◯◯◯ ◯◯◯◯◯

How to play: Complete the crossword puzzle by looking at the clues and unscrambling the answers. When the puzzle is complete, unscramble the circled letters to solve the BONUS.

JUMBLE® CROSSWORDS™

ACROSS

CLUE	ANSWER
1. Reverberated	HCDEEO
5. False	UBGOS
6. ______ cat	LAYEL
7. Called	HDPNOE

DOWN

CLUE	ANSWER
1. Symbol	BMMEEL
2. Untruth	HHSOAWG
3. A Greek letter	POSNEIL
4. Remained	TYDEAS

CLUE: "The last one I had was in an airport while I was waiting to catch a flight." D.L.H.

BONUS 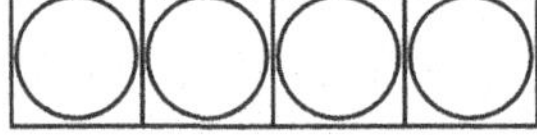 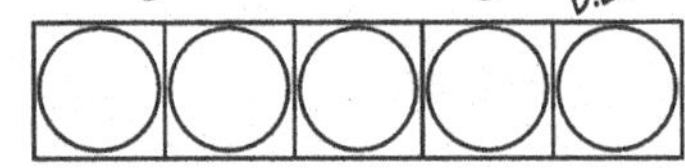

How to play: Complete the crossword puzzle by looking at the clues and unscrambling the answers. When the puzzle is complete, unscramble the circled letters to solve the BONUS.

ACROSS

CLUE	ANSWER
1. Space cloud	ANLEUB
5. ______ Island	LEISL
6. Cancels	DIVSO
7. Asian river	NGSEAG

DOWN

CLUE	ANSWER
1. Harass	ENEDEL
2. Home to Potosí	LIAOIBV
3. Long-______	ASNGLIT
4. Cooks	TAORSS

CLUE: Bear

BONUS

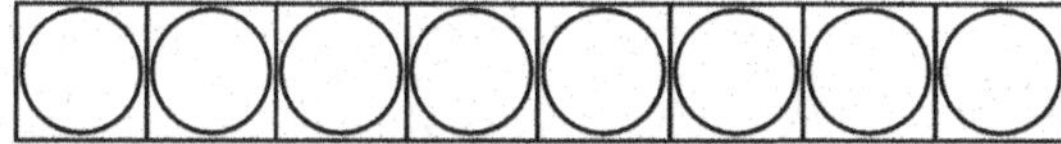

How to play: Complete the crossword puzzle by looking at the clues and unscrambling the answers. When the puzzle is complete, unscramble the circled letters to solve the BONUS.

JUMBLE® CROSSWORDS™

ACROSS

CLUE	ANSWER
1. Out of control	RYNLUU
5. Harbor	HANVE
6. Ships' parts	LKESE
7. Changed	DETDIE

DOWN

CLUE	ANSWER
1. Against difficulties	HULILP
2. Withdrawn	EEROVDK
3. Merciful	NEEITNL
4. ______ opportunity	DSMIES

CLUE: This comedic actress said, "I always wanted to be somebody, but I should have been more specific."

BONUS 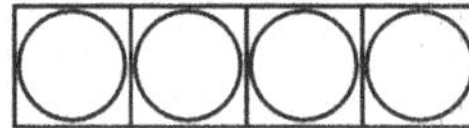 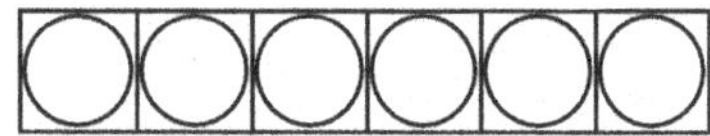

How to play: Complete the crossword puzzle by looking at the clues and unscrambling the answers. When the puzzle is complete, unscramble the circled letters to solve the BONUS.

JUMBLE® CROSSWORDS™

ACROSS

CLUE	ANSWER
1. Not wise	NIWESU
5. Controller	LPTIO
6. Gather	ASAMS
7. Water down	EKNEWA

DOWN

CLUE	ANSWER
1. Judge	PMIRUE
2. Mike ______	LAELCAW
3. Negative change	TKESCAB
4. ______ River	DOHUNS

CLUE: "Mine usually varies each day." D.L.H.

BONUS 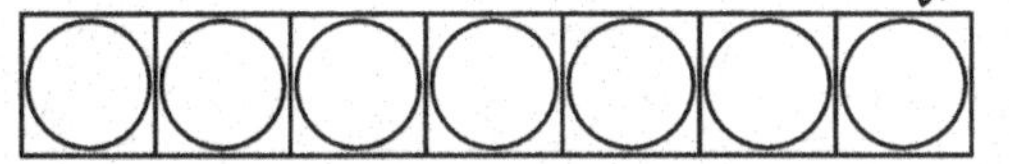

How to play: Complete the crossword puzzle by looking at the clues and unscrambling the answers. When the puzzle is complete, unscramble the circled letters to solve the BONUS.

#52

ACROSS

CLUE	ANSWER
1. Rotten	TPIURD
5. European city	RAISP
6. Stopped	DDEEN
7. Turbulent	MTRSOY

DOWN

CLUE	ANSWER
1. Type of tree	PPLORA
2. Deluge	RTERTNO
3. *The* ______	NEDISIR
4. Prosperous period	AEHYYD

CLUE: This country is divided into 76 provinces.

BONUS 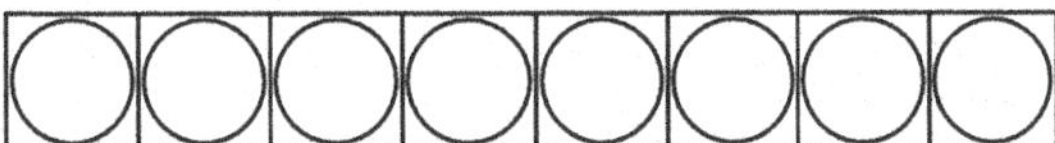

How to play — Complete the crossword puzzle by looking at the clues and unscrambling the answers. When the puzzle is complete, unscramble the circled letters to solve the BONUS.

ACROSS

CLUE	ANSWER
1. Yield	STMIBU
5. Prohibition	TOBAO
6. Dens	RSALI
7. Except	USSELN

DOWN

CLUE	ANSWER
1. House ______	TIESRT
2. Ancient city	NBYOLBA
3. Worship	IEZLOID
4. Body sections	WSATIS

CLUE: Tobacco is this country's principal cash crop.

BONUS

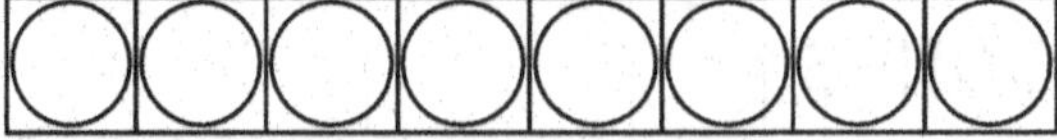

How to play: Complete the crossword puzzle by looking at the clues and unscrambling the answers. When the puzzle is complete, unscramble the circled letters to solve the BONUS.

JUMBLE® CROSSWORDS™

CLUE	ACROSS	ANSWER
1. Canine carnivore		LKAJCA
5. Shout of approval		ABORV
6. Remnants		ISNUR
7. Type of song		NAHMTE

CLUE	DOWN	ANSWER
1. Talk		ABREBJ
2. Distress of mind		RNIHGCA
3. Eliminate		OBLHIAS
4. Building material		PUGSMY

CLUE: This country is a parliamentary democracy governed under a 1962 constitution.

BONUS 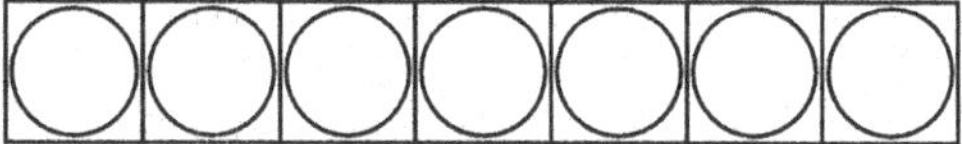

How to play: Complete the crossword puzzle by looking at the clues and unscrambling the answers. When the puzzle is complete, unscramble the circled letters to solve the BONUS.

ACROSS

CLUE	ANSWER
1. Unrestrained ruler	NRYATT
5. Number	DTIGI
6. Group of islands	ALTMA
7. Introduce as a factor	NTJIEC

DOWN

CLUE	ANSWER
1. Saunter	LDEOTD
2. Plan	GNEMRIE
3. ______ Portman	LITANAE
4. Pour off from the edge	NADETC

CLUE: This is up to 18 miles wide in some spots and is 277 miles long.

BONUS ○○○○○ ○○○○○○

How to play: Complete the crossword puzzle by looking at the clues and unscrambling the answers. When the puzzle is complete, unscramble the circled letters to solve the BONUS.

ACROSS

CLUE	ANSWER
1. Catchphrase	NGLASO
5. More	REATX
6. ______ check	NLKAB
7. Aspirations	MERDSA

DOWN

CLUE	ANSWER
1. Detective	HESTUL
2. "10"	ROECTOB
3. Home to Montgomery	BAAAALM
4. Small, loose parts	ELSKAF

CLUE: This member of the rodent family loves the water.

BONUS

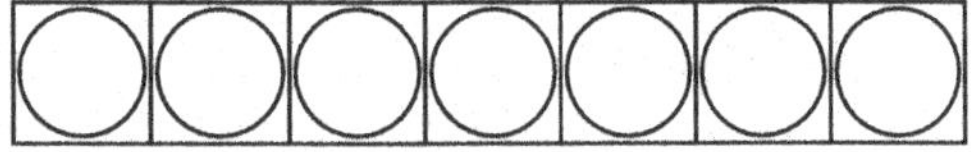

How to play: Complete the crossword puzzle by looking at the clues and unscrambling the answers. When the puzzle is complete, unscramble the circled letters to solve the BONUS.

JUMBLE® CROSSWORDS™

ACROSS

CLUE	ANSWER
1. Strike caller	PEIURM
5. Yellowish brown	KHAIK
6. A type of machine	TOORB
7. Room	YEWAEL

DOWN

CLUE	ANSWER
1. Mean	DNNUIK
2. ______ dog	RRIAIEP
3. A colorful display	AWRBNIO
4. Meritorious	HOTWRY

CLUE: This country is home to about 2.3 million people.

BONUS 

How to play Complete the crossword puzzle by looking at the clues and unscrambling the answers. When the puzzle is complete, unscramble the circled letters to solve the BONUS.

JUMBLE® CROSSWORDS™

ACROSS

CLUE	ANSWER
1. Hypothesis	RTOHEY
5. Separated	RPATA
6. One of fifty	HODAI
7. Together	DEINUT

DOWN

CLUE	ANSWER
1. Trails	ASCRKT
2. Tax ______	NISAVOE
3. Take back	RATRETC
4. Agreement	ACRDOC

CLUE: The ____ ____ lies at about 1,300 feet below sea level.

BONUS 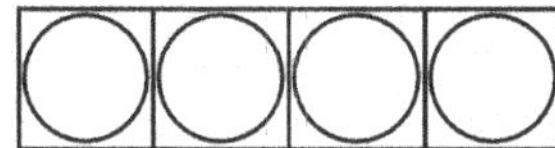 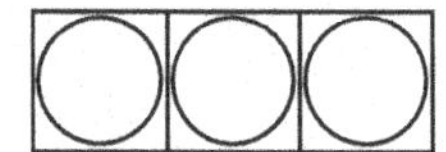

How to play — Complete the crossword puzzle by looking at the clues and unscrambling the answers. When the puzzle is complete, unscramble the circled letters to solve the BONUS.

JUMBLE® CROSSWORDS™

ACROSS

CLUE	ANSWER
1. New _____	YEEJSR
5. Rear	EIRAS
6. _____ of paper	TESEH
7. Japanese _____	ELETEB

DOWN

CLUE	ANSWER
1. 200-mile-long river	DOAJRN
2. Make available again	SERISUE
3. Trace _____	MELETNE
4. Dairy _____	ETCTLA

CLUE: This U.S. president fathered 15 children.

BONUS 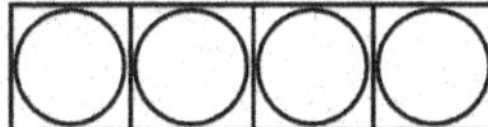 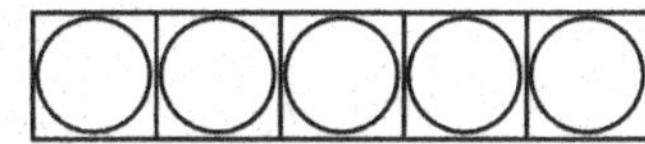

How to play: Complete the crossword puzzle by looking at the clues and unscrambling the answers. When the puzzle is complete, unscramble the circled letters to solve the BONUS.

JUMBLE® CROSSWORDS™

ACROSS

CLUE	ANSWER
1. Moving group	NCYOOV
5. American _____	ELAGE
6. To ridicule	ARTSO
7. Type of warning	VTAECA

DOWN

CLUE	ANSWER
1. Insensitive person	RICTEN
2. Home to Calabar	AINIREG
3. Run	EAPOETR
4. Type of group	PESTTE

CLUE: Donald Sutherland grew up in _____ _____.

BONUS 

How to play

Complete the crossword puzzle by looking at the clues and unscrambling the answers. When the puzzle is complete, unscramble the circled letters to solve the BONUS.

JUMBLE® CROSSWORDS™

ACROSS

CLUE	ANSWER
1. Fondly	LAEDYR
5. Black _____	DWWIO
6. Field _____	UMSOE
7. _____ Airlines	NTEIUD

DOWN

CLUE	ANSWER
1. Delay	WDELDA
2. Stomach area	DMONEAB
3. Type of case	ALSWITU
4. Story	NGEDEL

CLUE: This man is pictured on a 6¢ U.S. commemorative stamp.

BONUS  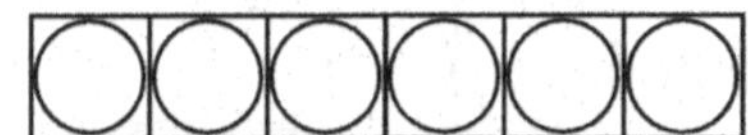

How to play: Complete the crossword puzzle by looking at the clues and unscrambling the answers. When the puzzle is complete, unscramble the circled letters to solve the BONUS.

CLUE	ACROSS	ANSWER
1. Among		MADTIS
5. Diminish		PTEAR
6. Primitive plant product		ERSOP
7. Mensch		SPNORE

CLUE	DOWN	ANSWER
1. Thoroughfare		TRAREY
2. Predicament		PSIEMAS
3. No-nonsense		SIEUSOR
4. Stool ______		NOEIPG

CLUE: These were successfully test-marketed in Cleveland, Ohio, in 1963.

BONUS 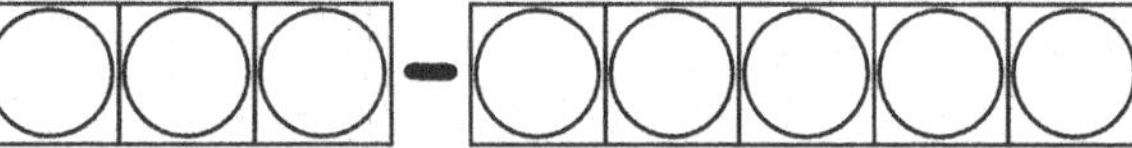

How to play: Complete the crossword puzzle by looking at the clues and unscrambling the answers. When the puzzle is complete, unscramble the circled letters to solve the BONUS.

ACROSS

CLUE	ANSWER
1. Frank	DDICNA
5. Taking ______	TNSOE
6. Allowable	ELGLA
7. Type of liquid	NRECAT

DOWN

CLUE	ANSWER
1. Core	TNEERC
2. ______ Cole	AALTNEI
3. Discernment	HSIGINT
4. Canadian ______	RADLOL

CLUE: Electrical ______ ______ were invented in 1892.

BONUS  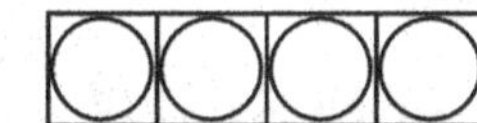

How to play: Complete the crossword puzzle by looking at the clues and unscrambling the answers. When the puzzle is complete, unscramble the circled letters to solve the BONUS.

ACROSS

CLUE	ANSWER
1. ______ time	LUOEBD
5. Stocky quadruped	BNIOS
6. Send	RITEM
7. Pain	NTIWEG

DOWN

CLUE	ANSWER
1. Remains	BIESDR
2. Open	USNWERC
3. Football player	AMNLEIN
4. ______ Beach	LEYTRM

CLUE: This man said, "I don't want to achieve immortality through my work; I want to achieve immortality through not dying."

BONUS

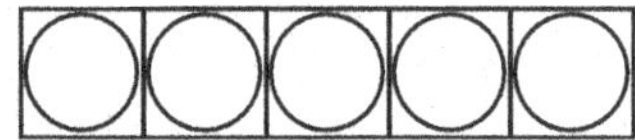

How to play: Complete the crossword puzzle by looking at the clues and unscrambling the answers. When the puzzle is complete, unscramble the circled letters to solve the BONUS.

JUMBLE CROSSWORDS™

ACROSS

CLUE	ANSWER
1. Volcanic glass	MUPEIC
5. _____ credit	AERTX
6. Registered _____	USNER
7. Tipped	DAELEN

DOWN

CLUE	ANSWER
1. Promise	DELGPE
2. Type of show	TAEMNIE
3. Much to her _____	AIGCRHN
4. Distribute	RSAEDP

CLUE: _____, _____, lies on the Manzanares River. It's situated on a vast, open plateau and is home to approximately 3.5 million people.

BONUS 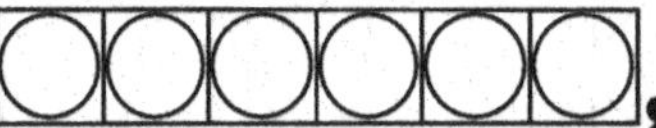, 

How to play: Complete the crossword puzzle by looking at the clues and unscrambling the answers. When the puzzle is complete, unscramble the circled letters to solve the BONUS.

JUMBLE® CROSSWORDS™

ACROSS CLUE	ANSWER
1. Injure	PRIMIA
5. Cats	NILOS
6. Pipe ______	ANOGR
7. Feverish	HCIETC

DOWN CLUE	ANSWER
1. Long ______	DINSAL
2. Incite	RVOPEOK
3. Seeing a situation	TISGNIH
4. ______ basket	NCICIP

CLUE: This man, who was born in 1899 in Brooklyn, New York, died in 1947.

BONUS  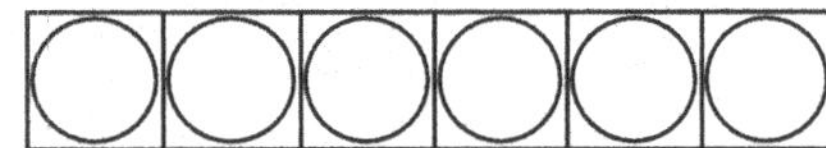

How to play: Complete the crossword puzzle by looking at the clues and unscrambling the answers. When the puzzle is complete, unscramble the circled letters to solve the BONUS.

ACROSS

CLUE	ANSWER
1. Jet _____	TASMER
5. Grand _____	ZPIER
6. Fade, faint	WONOS
7. Rubber _____	MECTNE

DOWN

CLUE	ANSWER
1. Pliant	PEUPSL
2. Publish again	EISERSU
3. Terrific	AMWOSEE
4. Nest builder	NHROET

CLUE: Oysters Rockefeller was invented in 1899 at Antoine's Restaurant in _____ _____.

BONUS  

How to play: Complete the crossword puzzle by looking at the clues and unscrambling the answers. When the puzzle is complete, unscramble the circled letters to solve the BONUS.

JUMBLE® CROSSWORDS™

ACROSS

CLUE	ANSWER
1. Quantum ______	RTYEHO
5. Advice	TNUIP
6. A, B, and C, but not H, I, and J	NSEOT
7. Fatal	DYDLAE

DOWN

CLUE	ANSWER
1. Adapt	RAOILT
2. Extent of land	AXSEENP
3. Turned	TOARDET
4. Numbered top	ESYRJE

CLUE: This woman was named one of *People* magazine's "50 Most Beautiful People in the World" in 1996.

BONUS 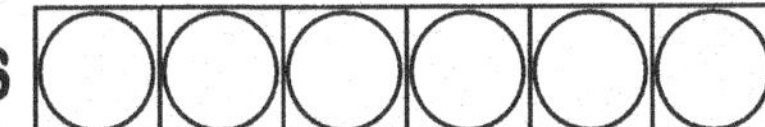 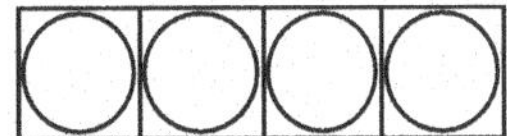

How to play: Complete the crossword puzzle by looking at the clues and unscrambling the answers. When the puzzle is complete, unscramble the circled letters to solve the BONUS.

ACROSS

CLUE	ANSWER
1. A Spanish explorer	AABBOL
5. Hard _____	DNAYC
6. Eject	PXELE
7. Thomas _____	EISNOD

DOWN

CLUE	ANSWER
1. _____ seats	KBTCUE
2. _____ oil	NILESDE
3. Mount _____	MYLOSUP
4. Legendary magician	RMNILE

CLUE: Steven Spielberg was offered a chance to direct this film, but the producers balked at his salary demands.

BONUS 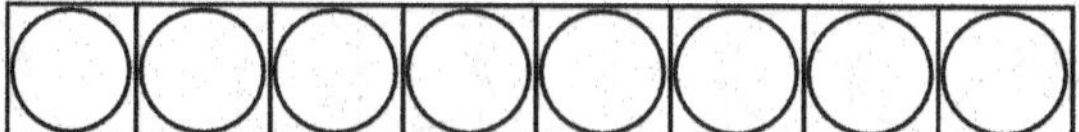

How to play: Complete the crossword puzzle by looking at the clues and unscrambling the answers. When the puzzle is complete, unscramble the circled letters to solve the BONUS.

JUMBLE® CROSSWORDS™

ACROSS

CLUE	ANSWER
1. Annually	YLYERA
5. ______ tree	MLNOE
6. First ______	ANSEM
7. Play subdivisions	NECSES

DOWN

CLUE	ANSWER
1. Screamed	LYEDEL
2. Type of publication	MCLANAA
3. Football position	ANILMEN
4. Sounds	NISEOS

CLUE: The ancient ______ made knives from volcanic glass.

BONUS 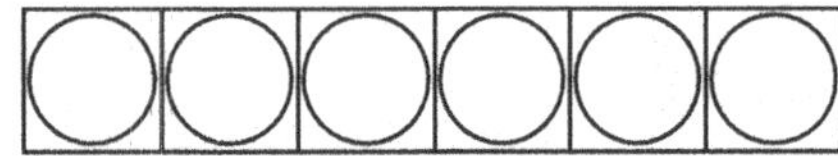

How to play — Complete the crossword puzzle by looking at the clues and unscrambling the answers. When the puzzle is complete, unscramble the circled letters to solve the BONUS.

JUMBLE® CROSSWORDS™

ACROSS

CLUE	ANSWER
1. _____ Cotten	POHJES
5. Type of seed	NAROC
6. Sluggish animal	AALOK
7. Nitty-_____	RTYGIT

DOWN

CLUE	ANSWER
1. _____ Cassidy	ANANOJ
2. Surprise	HCORSEK
3. Type of ornament	TPDNAEN
4. Disgrace	NYIFMA

CLUE: On his fourth voyage to the Americas, Columbus was marooned on _____ for more than a year.

BONUS 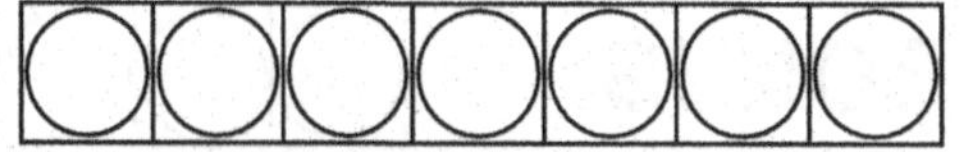

How to play: Complete the crossword puzzle by looking at the clues and unscrambling the answers. When the puzzle is complete, unscramble the circled letters to solve the BONUS.

JUMBLE® CROSSWORDS™

ACROSS

CLUE	ANSWER
1. Unsympathetic	DUNNIK
5. ______ light	TIPLO
6. L.L. TV show	LEAIC
7. American ______	AELEUG

DOWN

CLUE	ANSWER
1. Type of official	PMEIRU
2. TV doctor	LEIKADR
3. Zip	TNONHIG
4. Swindle	LFCEEE

CLUE: ______ Center consists of 19 buildings situated on 22 acres.

BONUS 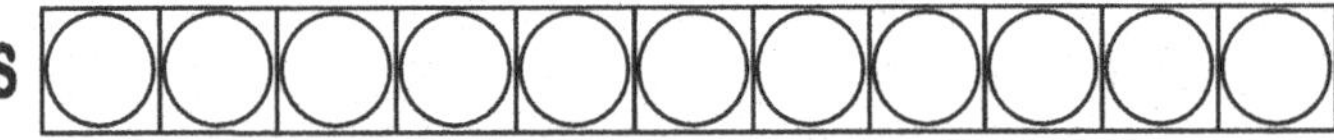

How to play: Complete the crossword puzzle by looking at the clues and unscrambling the answers. When the puzzle is complete, unscramble the circled letters to solve the BONUS.

#73

ACROSS

CLUE	ANSWER
1. Mutual	MNMOCO
5. Work out	EVSLO
6. Radioactive gas	NDOAR
7. Swampy	RTWYEA

DOWN

CLUE	ANSWER
1. Gambling building	ANOCIS
2. Type of disease	RIAALMA
3. Tardy	EVOREUD
4. Chiefly	YAIMLN

CLUE: Much of ______, ______, was destroyed by a fire in 1624.

BONUS 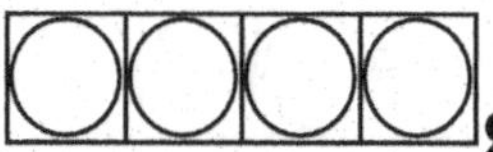 , 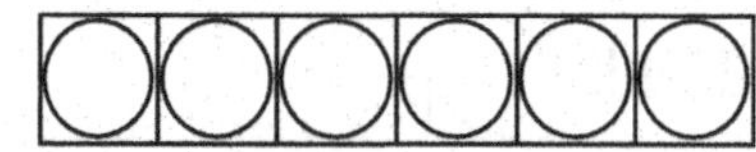

How to play: Complete the crossword puzzle by looking at the clues and unscrambling the answers. When the puzzle is complete, unscramble the circled letters to solve the BONUS.

JUMBLE® CROSSWORDS™

ACROSS

CLUE	ANSWER
1. A U.S. state capital	NAIUTS
5. Special _____	EGUTS
6. Home to Kisumu	KAYNE
7. Tribulation	DROLEA

DOWN

CLUE	ANSWER
1. Cornered	NEDALG
2. Talker	PSEKARE
3. Acute	TSNIEEN
4. Happen to	FLEABL

CLUE: The nest of a _____ _____ can weigh up to one ton.

BONUS  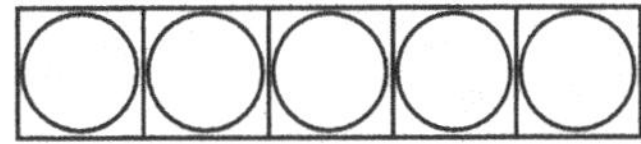

How to play: Complete the crossword puzzle by looking at the clues and unscrambling the answers. When the puzzle is complete, unscramble the circled letters to solve the BONUS.

JUMBLE® CROSSWORDS™

ACROSS

CLUE	ANSWER
1. Distinct article	UCALES
5. Competitor	RREAC
6. One in the background of a scene	ATXRE
7. Engraved	HECTDE

DOWN

CLUE	ANSWER
1. ______ Bernsen	RCNIOB
2. ______ history	NNTAEIC
3. Scrape	HSCCTAR
4. Mandate	MDNADE

CLUE: The United States launched its first ______ ______ in January 1954.

BONUS 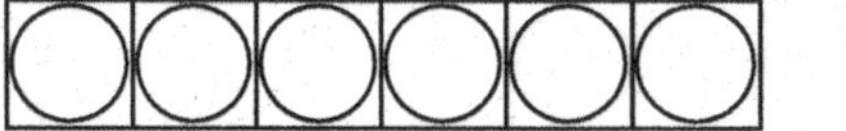 

How to play: Complete the crossword puzzle by looking at the clues and unscrambling the answers. When the puzzle is complete, unscramble the circled letters to solve the BONUS.

ACROSS

CLUE	ANSWER
1. Guanaco descendant	LCPAAA
5. Claude ______	NOMTE
6. Hunt	HEASC
7. Recently	TYELAL

DOWN

CLUE	ANSWER
1. Fleet	RAAMAD
2. Cure-all	NAEPCAA
3. ______ industry	TEGOCTA
4. Politely	NYLIEC

CLUE: The ______ were canceled in 1916, 1940, and 1944.

BONUS 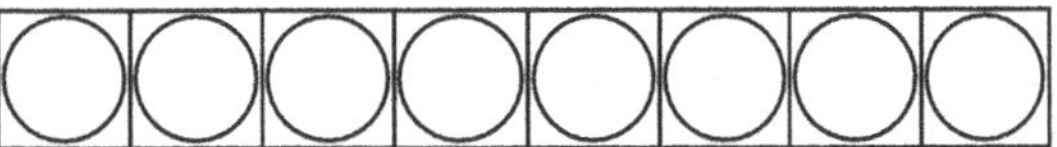

Complete the crossword puzzle by looking at the clues and

JUMBLE® CROSSWORDS™

ACROSS

CLUE	ANSWER
1. Said	EPNSKO
5. Exchange _____	TRESA
6. _____ change	XCATE
7. Rests	PLSSEE

DOWN

CLUE	ANSWER
1. Leave on base	TRSDNA
2. _____ cookie	LOTAAEM
3. Catch	NSEANER
4. Composes	RIWEST

CLUE: This former professional soccer player was inducted into the Rock and Roll Hall of Fame in 1994.

BONUS  

How to play: Complete the crossword puzzle by looking at the clues and unscrambling the answers. When the puzzle is complete, unscramble the circled letters to solve the BONUS.

ACROSS

CLUE	ANSWER
1. A unit of measure	NIORCM
5. Unite	YUFIN
6. ______ cut	PPREA
7. Off-______	ASOENS

DOWN

CLUE	ANSWER
1. Mangled	ALUDEM
2. Maim	RICPLEP
3. Mount ______	YLPMSOU
4. Customer	TOPNRA

CLUE: ______ is about the same size as Maine.

BONUS 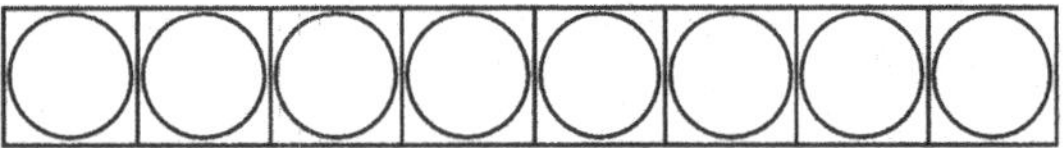

How to play: Complete the crossword puzzle by looking at the clues and unscrambling the answers. When the puzzle is complete, unscramble the circled letters to solve the BONUS.

JUMBLE® CROSSWORDS™

CLUE	ACROSS	ANSWER
1. Force		RCCEEO
5. Historic philosopher		ALPOT
6. Invited		KSADE
7. Male or female		NGREED

CLUE	DOWN	ANSWER
1. Reproductions		PCEIOS
2. Spring from		MAAENET
3. Concealed		LOKADEC
4. Type of plane		DRILGE

CLUE: The _____ Islands were discovered in 1535 by the Spanish navigator Tomás de Berlanga.

BONUS 

How to play: Complete the crossword puzzle by looking at the clues and unscrambling the answers. When the puzzle is complete, unscramble the circled letters to solve the BONUS.

ACROSS

CLUE	ANSWER
1. African ______	LEOIVT
5. ______ pipe	ETWAS
6. To a specified time	NITUL
7. Writing styles	RNEEGS

DOWN

CLUE	ANSWER
1. A and O, for example	WOEVSL
2. Cryptic	BSOUCER
3. ______ set	RECEROT
4. Calcareous coverings	LELHSS

CLUE: This "rock collection" dates back thousands of years.

BONUS 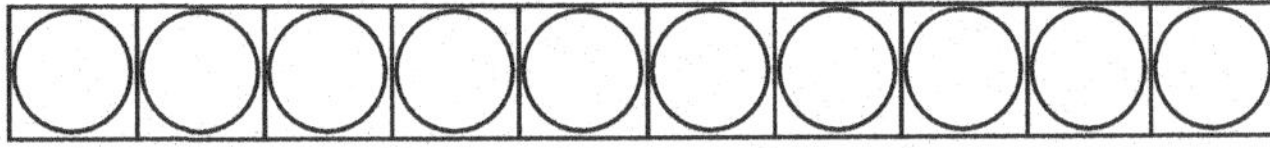

How to play: Complete the crossword puzzle by looking at the clues and unscrambling the answers. When the puzzle is complete, unscramble the circled letters to solve the BONUS.

JUMBLE CROSSWORDS™

ACROSS

CLUE	ANSWER
1. Pact	REYTAT
5. A heart, for example	NOARG
6. Picture within a picture	TIESN
7. Cuts	ESASRH

DOWN

CLUE	ANSWER
1. Type of hand tool	LOTERW
2. Body ______	HNESIGL
3. African country	NIATIUS
4. Free	SGIRTA

CLUE: On average, this kills about 73 people annually in the United States.

BONUS 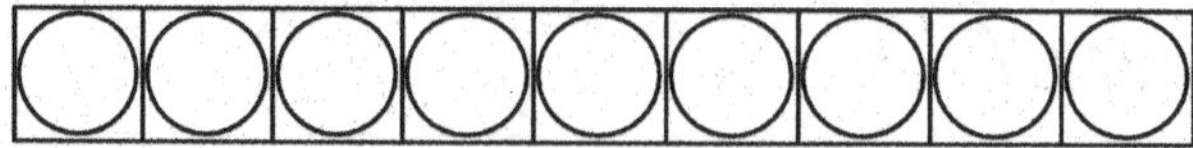

How to play: Complete the crossword puzzle by looking at the clues and unscrambling the answers. When the puzzle is complete, unscramble the circled letters to solve the BONUS.

JUMBLE® CROSSWORDS™

ACROSS

CLUE	ANSWER
1. Pair	PULOEC
5. ______ Dern	RAUAL
6. Credit ______	UINNO
7. Plant disease	LTBGIH

DOWN

CLUE	ANSWER
1. Phoned	LCDELA
2. Different	USANLUU
3. Slanting	AIELNGN
4. ______ school	TNGAEM

CLUE: The ______ alphabet has more than 70 letters.

BONUS ◯◯◯◯◯◯◯◯◯

How to play: Complete the crossword puzzle by looking at the clues and unscrambling the answers. When the puzzle is complete, unscramble the circled letters to solve the BONUS.

ACROSS

CLUE	ANSWER
1. Joined	THICDEH
5. Open	NPACU
6. Incompetent	PTINE
7. Eats	ESITNSG

DOWN

CLUE	ANSWER
1. Harry ______	UIOHIDN
2. Loose stitches	KAGITNC
3. Luckless	PSASHEL
4. Gives	NEDTASO

CLUE: There are about nine hundred thousand species of these.

BONUS 

How to play: Complete the crossword puzzle by looking at the clues and unscrambling the answers. When the puzzle is complete, unscramble the circled letters to solve the BONUS.

JUMBLE® CROSSWORDS™

ACROSS

CLUE	ANSWER
1. Square root of 225	NFEIEFT
5. Springs	LCIOS
6. Lets slip	ELTSL
7. Contracts	NIRSSKH

DOWN

CLUE	ANSWER
1. Components	ACRSFOT
2. Apple ______	RITFRTE
3. A Greek letter	ELINOSP
4. Camp attendees	DNISSTU

CLUE: Finding words that rhyme with *month* and *orange*, for example.

BONUS 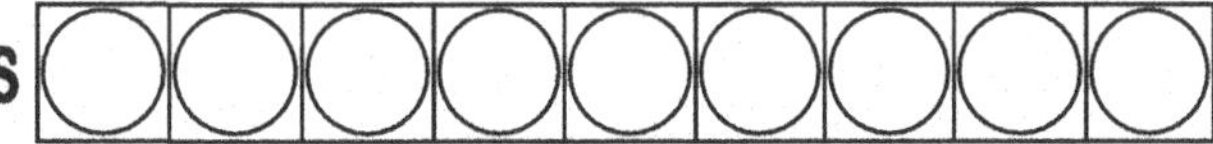

How to play: Complete the crossword puzzle by looking at the clues and unscrambling the answers. When the puzzle is complete, unscramble the circled letters to solve the BONUS.

JUMBLE® CROSSWORDS™

ACROSS

CLUE	ANSWER
1. Plan	HEECSM
5. Type of hit	MOHRE
6. Cord	EIWNT
7. Good _____	RAGSED

DOWN

CLUE	ANSWER
1. Summer _____	HOCSLO
2. Short-tailed animal	MAHTSRE
3. Hitched	DERAIRM
4. 1986 S.W. movie	LAEISN

CLUE: This TV show was rated number two four times but never reached the top spot.

BONUS

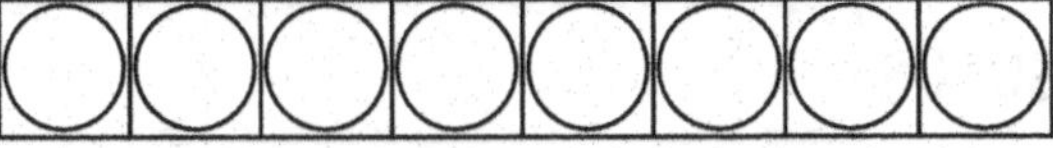

How to play: Complete the crossword puzzle by looking at the clues and unscrambling the answers. When the puzzle is complete, unscramble the circled letters to solve the BONUS.

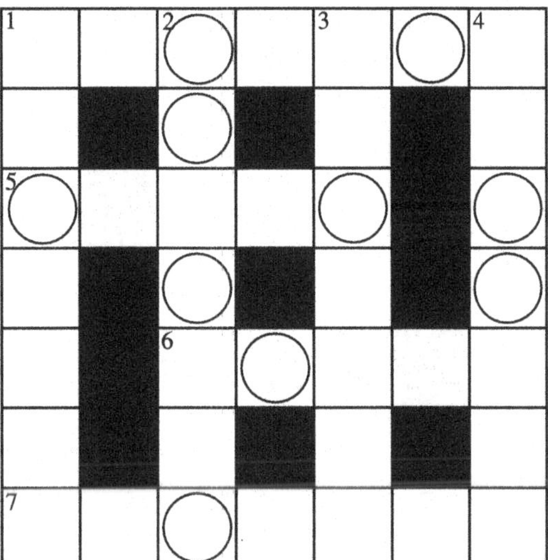

ACROSS

CLUE	ANSWER
1. Freehanded	ABLREIL
5. A titan	LTSAA
6. Type of group	TCOTE
7. Elders or some students	NSIREOS

DOWN

CLUE	ANSWER
1. Hates	AOLHTSE
2. Weather ______	LBOLNOA
3. Rice dish	TOTSIRO
4. Finds	ETACSOL

CLUE: This city was almost completely destroyed by an earthquake in 1755.

BONUS 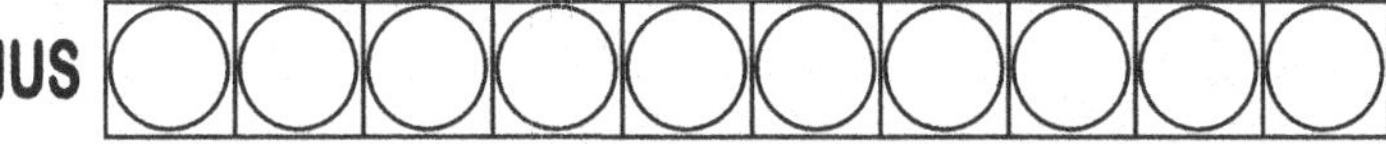

How to play — Complete the crossword puzzle by looking at the clues and unscrambling the answers. When the puzzle is complete, unscramble the circled letters to solve the BONUS.

JUMBLE® CROSSWORDS™

ACROSS CLUE	ANSWER
1. Type of killer	LIRAAAM
5. ______ by a bee	TGNUS
6. Coins	MEDIS
7. Holy places	ERSSNIH

DOWN CLUE	ANSWER
1. Out of place people	TISMFIS
2. Clean	LREDNUA
3. Systematic plan	MEGRINE
4. Aligns	DTAJSUS

CLUE: This takes up about 23 square miles.

BONUS 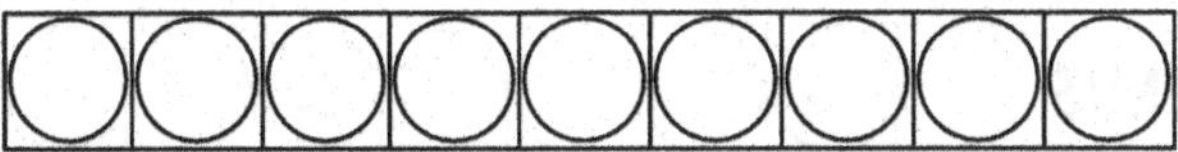

How to play: Complete the crossword puzzle by looking at the clues and unscrambling the answers. When the puzzle is complete, unscramble the circled letters to solve the BONUS.

JUMBLE® CROSSWORDS™

ACROSS	
CLUE	**ANSWER**
1. Ominous	LRIDFEU
5. Saying	TOMTO
6. Switch	REDTA
7. Sorrow	DSASESN

DOWN	
CLUE	**ANSWER**
1. Hurts	MGDASEA
2. Turned	TAERTOD
3. Series of shots	TOAOGFE
4. Unruly	WLESALS

CLUE: In 1975 this actor graduated from Western Michigan University with a degree in television production.

BONUS 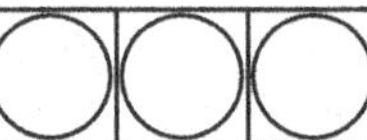 

How to play: Complete the crossword puzzle by looking at the clues and unscrambling the answers. When the puzzle is complete, unscramble the circled letters to solve the BONUS.

JUMBLE® CROSSWORDS™

ACROSS

CLUE	ANSWER
1. Animal ______	KARCREC
5. ______ade	MELNO
6. Home to Birganj	ELPNA
7. Bridged	DPNSNEA

DOWN

CLUE	ANSWER
1. L.B.'s old team	LECSCIT
2. ______ water	MIAMANO
3. W.H. movie	NKIGIPN
4. Discomposed	UERFLDF

CLUE: This person, who died in 1945, said, "I keep my ideals, because in spite of everything, I still believe that people are really good at heart."

BONUS 

How to play: Complete the crossword puzzle by looking at the clues and unscrambling the answers. When the puzzle is complete, unscramble the circled letters to solve the BONUS.

JUMBLE CROSSWORDS™

ACROSS

CLUE	ANSWER
1. Ratify	MRFAIF
5. Pig _____	TIALN
6. Luxury	RLFIL
7. _____ deck	HLTFIG

DOWN

CLUE	ANSWER
1. On fire	LBZAAE
2. Portentous	TAFFLUE
3. Raving	NARITGN
4. Type of youngster	PETILG

CLUE: Begin

BONUS 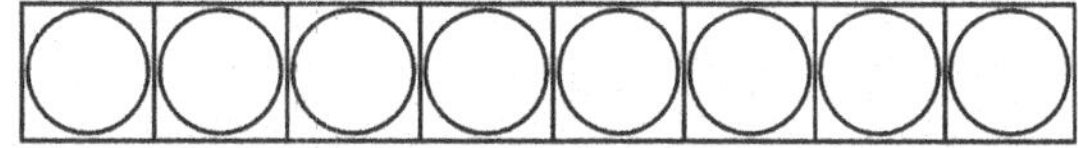

How to play: Complete the crossword puzzle by looking at the clues and unscrambling the answers. When the puzzle is complete, unscramble the circled letters to solve the BONUS.

JUMBLE CROSSWORDS™

ACROSS

CLUE	ANSWER
1. Rightful	ALLFUW
5. Group	RAWSM
6. Turn	PTIOV
7. _____ check	ERCTID

DOWN

CLUE	ANSWER
1. Finally	ASLYLT
2. Cover	RAWPREP
3. Indifferent to emotion	NDVMUEO
4. Consists of seven voices	PESTTE

CLUE: This woman said, "It's not the men in your life that count, it's the life in your men."

BONUS 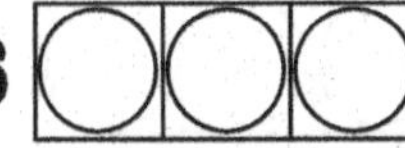 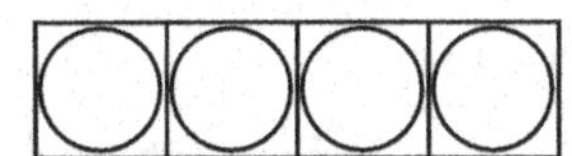

How to play: Complete the crossword puzzle by looking at the clues and unscrambling the answers. When the puzzle is complete, unscramble the circled letters to solve the BONUS.

JUMBLE® CROSSWORDS™

ACROSS

CLUE	ANSWER
1. Untidy place	TPYISG
5. Home to Nakuru	NEKAY
6. Comment	PNITU
7. Close	ANEBRY

DOWN

CLUE	ANSWER
1. ______ duck	KGEPIN
2. Real	NNUGIEE
3. W.R. role	REPRATP
4. Weakly	FOTSYL

CLUE: This country is about the same size as Indiana (approximately thirty-five thousand square miles).

BONUS 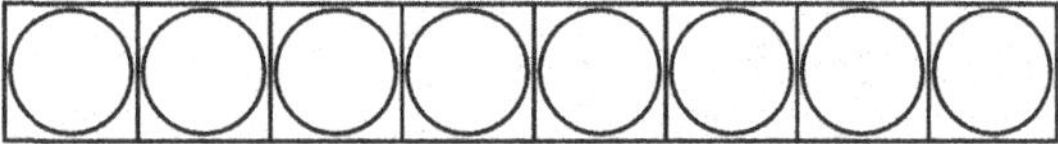

How to play: Complete the crossword puzzle by looking at the clues and unscrambling the answers. When the puzzle is complete, unscramble the circled letters to solve the BONUS.

ACROSS

CLUE	ANSWER
1. Small	TPIEET
5. _____ out	HLILC
6. Sure _____	HNGIT
7. Connector	DIRBEG

DOWN

CLUE	ANSWER
1. Dilemma	LCIEKP
2. Type of storm	RWTISET
3. Added up	LTILDEA
4. Animal grouping	ALEGGG

CLUE: This U.S. state capital is home to about two hundred thousand people.

BONUS

How to play: Complete the crossword puzzle by looking at the clues and unscrambling the answers. When the puzzle is complete, unscramble the circled letters to solve the BONUS.

JUMBLE® CROSSWORDS™

ACROSS

CLUE	ANSWER
1. Attention-getting	TCHAYC
5. Vex	NYAON
6. Lift	ISREA
7. To be imminent	DEPMIN

DOWN

CLUE	ANSWER
1. Drawing stick	NYORAC
2. Fit	UMRTNTA
3. Crazy	AWREIYH
4. Bud	NRIEDF

CLUE: This country is larger than Texas but smaller than Alaska.

BONUS

How to play: Complete the crossword puzzle by looking at the clues and unscrambling the answers. When the puzzle is complete, unscramble the circled letters to solve the BONUS.

JUMBLE® CROSSWORDS™

ACROSS

CLUE	ANSWER
1. Reckless	CDMAPA
5. Silent _____	VOIME
6. Jumped	APTLE
7. Disbelief, dissent	ESYREH

DOWN

CLUE	ANSWER
1. Instant	TMNMEO
2. Tell	GVIDUEL
3. Customary	ERAEAVG
4. Deserving	HOTYWR

CLUE: The first coin-operated vending machines in the United States dispensed this.

BONUS  

How to play: Complete the crossword puzzle by looking at the clues and unscrambling the answers. When the puzzle is complete, unscramble the circled letters to solve the BONUS.

JUMBLE® CROSSWORDS™

CLUE	ACROSS	ANSWER
1. ______ Christie		AHTAAG
5. Chambers		MSORO
6. A cold dome		OLIOG
7. Coastal areas		SRESOH

CLUE	DOWN	ANSWER
1. Fearful		IARDAF
2. Annul		LOSBHIA
3. Swindler		RLETSUH
4. Streams		KORSBO

CLUE: These are found all along United States highways.

BONUS 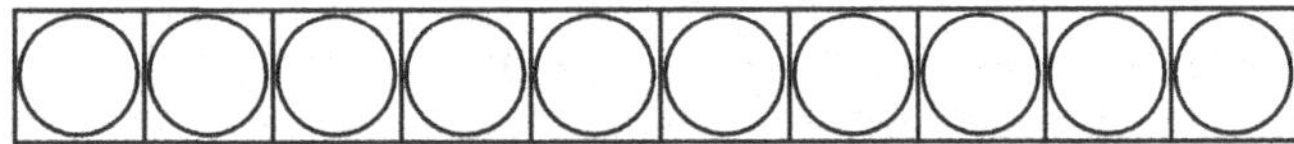

How to play Complete the crossword puzzle by looking at the clues and unscrambling the answers. When the puzzle is complete, unscramble the circled letters to solve the BONUS.

ACROSS

CLUE	ANSWER
1. Asian structure	DGOAPA
5. January, for example	SITRF
6. Style	LIRFA
7. Space _____	RETHAE

DOWN

CLUE	ANSWER
1. Type of seabird	FUIFNP
2. The tallest of its kind	FERGIFA
3. Diminish	CTDERTA
4. Closer	REERAN

CLUE: The _____ is made up of 12 provinces.

BONUS

How to play: Complete the crossword puzzle by looking at the clues and unscrambling the answers. When the puzzle is complete, unscramble the circled letters to solve the BONUS.

ACROSS

CLUE	ANSWER
1. A type of garment	RIADEP
5. Ranked	DTERA
6. Playing _____	DRASC
7. Gems	WLESJE

DOWN

CLUE	ANSWER
1. Compulsion by threat	SRESUD
2. _____ case	HTACETA
3. Approve	EDORNES
4. Home to Lawrence	ASNASK

CLUE: Nosocomephobia is the fear of _____.

BONUS 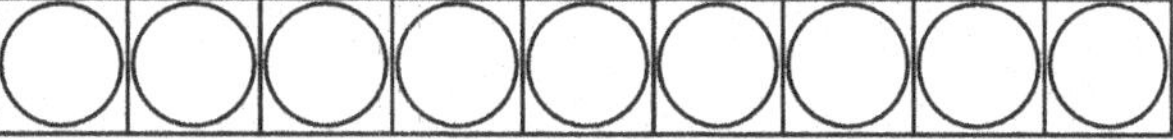

How to play: Complete the crossword puzzle by looking at the clues and unscrambling the answers. When the puzzle is complete, unscramble the circled letters to solve the BONUS.

JUMBLE® CROSSWORDS™

ACROSS

CLUE	ANSWER
1. ______ fuel	ESILED
5. Course	URTEO
6. ______ Empire	ZECTA
7. ______ bender	NRDEEF

DOWN

CLUE	ANSWER
1. Charles ______	AWNIRD
2. Inform	ECEDTAU
3. Picked	DECETLE
4. Agree	NCROUC

CLUE: No settlement in this country is more than 75 miles from the sea.

BONUS ○○○ ○○○○○○○

How to play: Complete the crossword puzzle by looking at the clues and unscrambling the answers. When the puzzle is complete, unscramble the circled letters to solve the BONUS.

JUMBLE® CROSSWORDS™

ACROSS

CLUE	ANSWER
1. Repeat from memory	ETRICE
5. ______ weave	TNIAS
6. Doctrine	MDAGO
7. Overjoyed	ADLETE

DOWN

CLUE	ANSWER
1. Vacation spot	TESRRO
2. Fortress	EDLATIC
3. *The ______ Show*	NGTOHIT
4. Home to Gdynia	DAOPNL

CLUE: This man was a prizefighter, steel mill laborer, and gas station attendant before seeing his first glimmer of fame.

BONUS 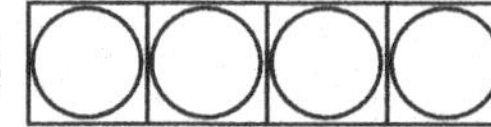 

How to play Complete the crossword puzzle by looking at the clues and unscrambling the answers. When the puzzle is complete, unscramble the circled letters to solve the BONUS.

JUMBLE® CROSSWORDS™

ACROSS

CLUE	ANSWER
1. _____ circle	AFRTCIF
5. Type of reptile	EOKCG
6. Home to Gonaïves	AITIH
7. Press _____	LSEAEER

DOWN

CLUE	ANSWER
1. Closer	EITRHTG
2. Grain _____	LLHOOAC
3. South _____	ARLIODF
4. Poisonous compound	DNAIYCE

CLUE: This U.S. president was born in Ohio.

BONUS

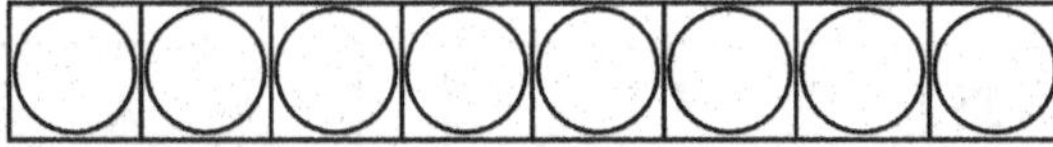

How to play: Complete the crossword puzzle by looking at the clues and unscrambling the answers. When the puzzle is complete, unscramble the circled letters to solve the BONUS.

#102

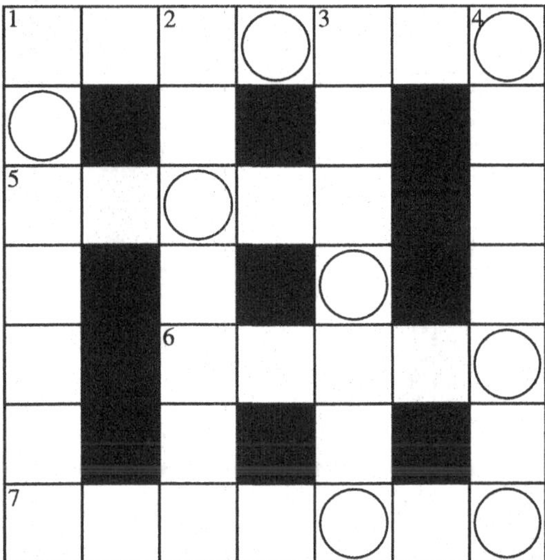

ACROSS

CLUE	ANSWER
1. Loyal	TVEEDOD
5. The 24th of its kind	MAGEO
6. Half _____	TSEON
7. Comments	RERASKM

DOWN

CLUE	ANSWER
1. Medicine _____	PORRDEP
2. South _____	EITMVAN
3. Type of machine	RRATOCT
4. Hates	DSTTESE

CLUE: The American _____ _____ was organized in 1881.

BONUS  

How to play: Complete the crossword puzzle by looking at the clues and unscrambling the answers. When the puzzle is complete, unscramble the circled letters to solve the BONUS.

JUMBLE® CROSSWORDS™

ACROSS

CLUE	ANSWER
1. Divide	TBCIES
5. Celestial formation	OONIR
6. Tall grasses	ESDER
7. Indifference	YHAAPT

DOWN

CLUE	ANSWER
1. Creeks	KROBSO
2. Foot frame	TSIPURR
3. Join	NOCENTC
4. Dump	YTSIPG

CLUE: _____ _____ were introduced in 1929.

BONUS 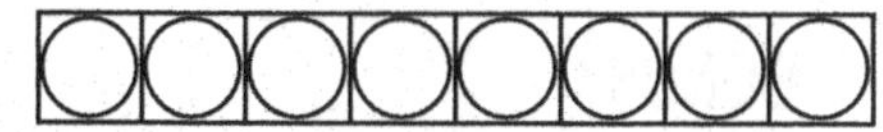

How to play: Complete the crossword puzzle by looking at the clues and unscrambling the answers. When the puzzle is complete, unscramble the circled letters to solve the BONUS.

JUMBLE® CROSSWORDS™

CLUE	ACROSS	ANSWER
1. Stylish		YSPNPA
5. Breed		RSEIA
6. ______ Mountains		ARKZO
7. Defective		YAFUTL

CLUE	DOWN	ANSWER
1. ______ light		BESORT
2. Home to Yuma		NRAAIOZ
3. Win		EVLARIP
4. Gently, humbly		MEYLKE

CLUE: This automobile pioneer lived from 1844 to 1929.

BONUS

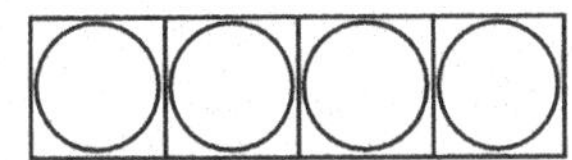

How to play: Complete the crossword puzzle by looking at the clues and unscrambling the answers. When the puzzle is complete, unscramble the circled letters to solve the BONUS.

JUMBLE® CROSSWORDS™

ACROSS

CLUE	ANSWER
1. Easily	EFERYL
5. Elongated creatures	WSMRO
6. Revel selfishly	TGAOL
7. Thomas _____	NEISOD

DOWN

CLUE	ANSWER
1. Least	EFETWS
2. Angered	RENEADG
3. Ropes	ASLOSES
4. Tiny "+"	NPOORT

CLUE: This woman said, "I'm not offended by dumb blonde jokes because I know that I'm not dumb. I also know I'm not blonde."

BONUS  

How to play Complete the crossword puzzle by looking at the clues and unscrambling the answers. When the puzzle is complete, unscramble the circled letters to solve the BONUS.

JUMBLE® CROSSWORDS™

ACROSS

CLUE	ANSWER
1. Temple	AOADGP
5. Safety _____	ZRRAO
6. Seventh sign	BALIR
7. Duplicity	DECITE

DOWN

CLUE	ANSWER
1. Spoof	YRDAOP
2. Graceful animal	LZEGLEA
3. Lasting	EDLUBAR
4. Retract	TECRAN

CLUE: _____, _____, is home to about 7 million people. It was founded in 969. Tourism is important to its economy.

BONUS , 

How to play: Complete the crossword puzzle by looking at the clues and unscrambling the answers. When the puzzle is complete, unscramble the circled letters to solve the BONUS.

JUMBLE® CROSSWORDS™

ACROSS

CLUE	ANSWER
1. Timothy Hutton movie	NACIME
5. Topic of discourse	EEMTH
6. _____ box	LOEGV
7. Beginning	DVEATN

DOWN

CLUE	ANSWER
1. _____ valve	KEAINT
2. Came into view	EEDRMEG
3. Great	AMWOSEE
4. Affirm	TESTTA

CLUE: At one point most homes in the United States had one, but now fewer than 50 percent do.

BONUS 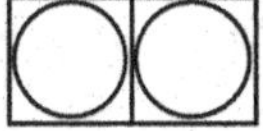 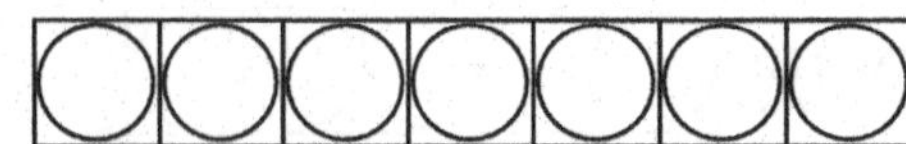

How to play — Complete the crossword puzzle by looking at the clues and unscrambling the answers. When the puzzle is complete, unscramble the circled letters to solve the BONUS.

JUMBLE® CROSSWORDS™

ACROSS

CLUE	ANSWER
1. Subjects	HEETSM
5. Weasel family member	ALSEB
6. Wear away	ROEED
7. Conducts to a place	ESRSHU

DOWN

CLUE	ANSWER
1. ______ paper	TSUSIE
2. Insignias	BELMSEM
3. Unattractive sight	ESEYREO
4. Consents	RGAESE

CLUE: The U.S. ______ Service was founded on August 7, 1789.

BONUS 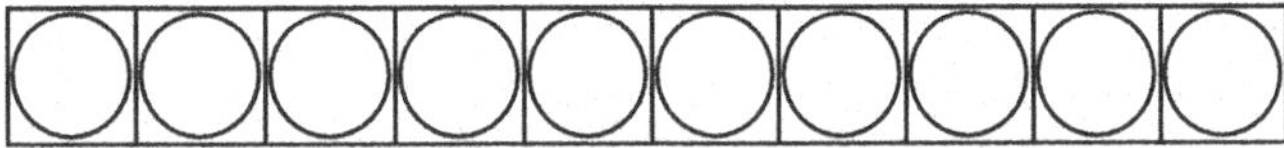

How to play: Complete the crossword puzzle by looking at the clues and unscrambling the answers. When the puzzle is complete, unscramble the circled letters to solve the BONUS.

JUMBLE® CROSSWORDS™

CLUE	ACROSS	ANSWER
1. Emerge		RAEPAP
5. Suffocate		KHOEC
6. Large seed		NRCAO
7. Cure		MYEERD

CLUE	DOWN	ANSWER
1. Rise		DANECS
2. ______ court		RTBEPOA
3. Amazing		AMOWEES
4. Chiefly		YAIMLN

CLUE: The first ______ ______ was issued by the U.S. government in 1862.

BONUS 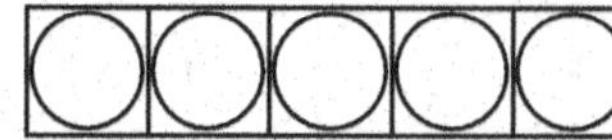 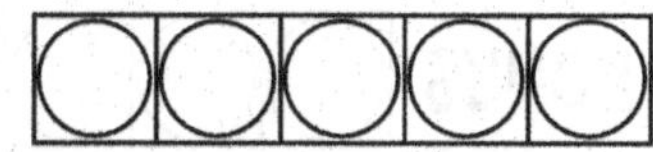

How to play: Complete the crossword puzzle by looking at the clues and unscrambling the answers. When the puzzle is complete, unscramble the circled letters to solve the BONUS.

JUMBLE® CROSSWORDS™

ACROSS

CLUE	ANSWER
1. One-piece outfit	PURJEM
5. ______ butter	AOOCC
6. Corrections	DESIT
7. Menace	RHTATE

DOWN

CLUE	ANSWER
1. Coat	KECTAJ
2. Scottish character	BCEATMH
3. Canvass	MAEEINX
4. ______ hound	TSBEAS

CLUE: In 1951 ____ ____ ____ ____ opened its first restaurant in San Diego, California, pioneering the drive-through concept and featuring 18¢ hamburgers.

BONUS 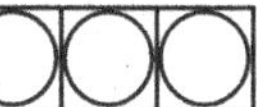   

How to play — Complete the crossword puzzle by looking at the clues and unscrambling the answers. When the puzzle is complete, unscramble the circled letters to solve the BONUS.

JUMBLE® CROSSWORDS™

ACROSS

CLUE	ANSWER
1. Quick	MRTPOP
5. Up to	TINUL
6. Type of scarf	ATOSC
7. Speed _____	KTASRE

DOWN

CLUE	ANSWER
1. Spirited	PCUYKL
2. Australian region	TKUBAOC
3. Type of mammal	LEOPCTA
4. Air _____	URIGTA

CLUE: In 1400 B.C., it was the fashion among rich _____ women to place a large cone of scented grease on top of their heads.

BONUS 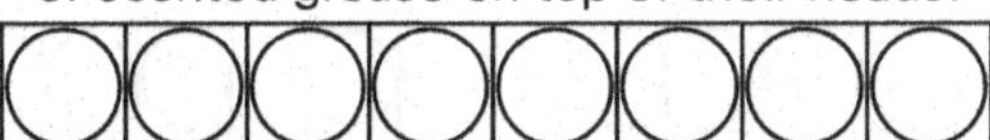

How to play: Complete the crossword puzzle by looking at the clues and unscrambling the answers. When the puzzle is complete, unscramble the circled letters to solve the BONUS.

JUMBLE® CROSSWORDS™

CLUE	ACROSS	ANSWER
1. Believe		PCECAT
5. Distant orbiter		TLUOP
6. Change		MDEAN
7. Type of top		RYJEES

CLUE	DOWN	ANSWER
1. Granny Smiths		PALPSE
2. Military expedition		RCSUEAD
3. Declare		POSEFSR
4. Courteously		NILYDK

CLUE: On June 22, 1870, the U.S. Congress created the Department of ______.

BONUS 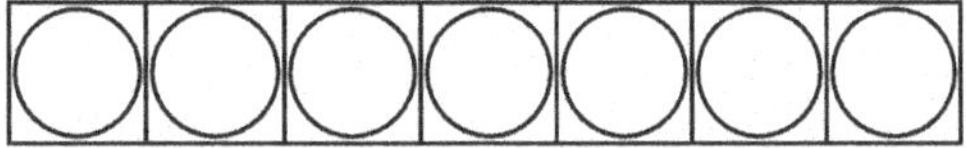

How to play: Complete the crossword puzzle by looking at the clues and unscrambling the answers. When the puzzle is complete, unscramble the circled letters to solve the BONUS.

JUMBLE® CROSSWORDS™

ACROSS

CLUE	ANSWER
1. Type of hawk	ROPESY
5. Crack	FLETC
6. Legislate	TENCA
7. Said	DESATT

DOWN

CLUE	ANSWER
1. Type of plant	DCORIH
2. Current	NESTEPR
3. Educe	RETATXC
4. Endured	ADLEST

CLUE: _____, _____, was founded in the mid-1800s. Many of the new settlers were French immigrants from the failed colony La Reunion.

BONUS  , 

How to play: Complete the crossword puzzle by looking at the clues and unscrambling the answers. When the puzzle is complete, unscramble the circled letters to solve the BONUS.

JUMBLE® CROSSWORDS™

ACROSS

CLUE	ANSWER
1. ______ Dam	RUOLBED
5. Slides	KDISS
6. Alpha and ______	MOEAG
7. Gave	TANDDOE

DOWN

CLUE	ANSWER
1. Moved briskly	UEDBLTS
2. Mythical animal	NRUICON
3. Analyze	TDCIESS
4. Gere or Hatch	RIDRHCA

CLUE: There are about 32 species of these, and all of them are venomous.

BONUS  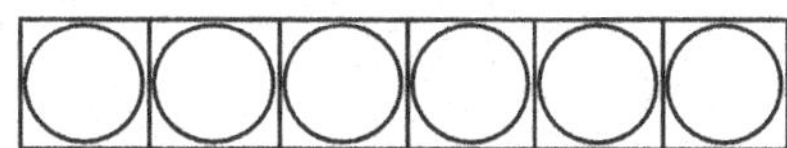

How to play: Complete the crossword puzzle by looking at the clues and unscrambling the answers. When the puzzle is complete, unscramble the circled letters to solve the BONUS.

JUMBLE® CROSSWORDS™

CLUE	ACROSS	ANSWER
1. A teaching method		NPHOCIS
5. Fence doors		TGSAE
6. Dinner and lunch		LMESA
7. U.S. or state _____		RSOETAN

CLUE	DOWN	ANSWER
1. Short-tailed youngsters		TISPELG
2. _____ Empire		NTOMOTA
3. _____ coffee		ANISTTN
4. Supporter		PORSSNO

CLUE: Mischievous activities

BONUS ◯◯◯◯◯◯◯◯◯◯◯

How to play: Complete the crossword puzzle by looking at the clues and unscrambling the answers. When the puzzle is complete, unscramble the circled letters to solve the BONUS.

JUMBLE® CROSSWORDS™

ACROSS

CLUE	ANSWER
1. Style of music	ETGIARM
5. Mass of vapor	DOCUL
6. Upright ____	NIPAO
7. Exceed	PSSRUSA

DOWN

CLUE	ANSWER
1. Gets back	EPSROUC
2. Large ocean fish	ROGUREP
3. Home to Gary	NDIAAIN
4. Proofreaders	TIOESRD

CLUE: ____ has the world's highest number of livestock per person.

BONUS

How to play: Complete the crossword puzzle by looking at the clues and unscrambling the answers. When the puzzle is complete, unscramble the circled letters to solve the BONUS.

JUMBLE® CROSSWORDS™

ACROSS

CLUE	ANSWER
1. Indian child	PPOEASO
5. Encircle	BIROT
6. Strings	AESLC
7. Forced	LCSDMEU

DOWN

CLUE	ANSWER
1. Show	RMOPRGA
2. Small stones	EESPLBB
3. ______ fiber	PATOCIL
4. Passed	PALEDSE

CLUE: This word's origin dates back to about the second century.

BONUS 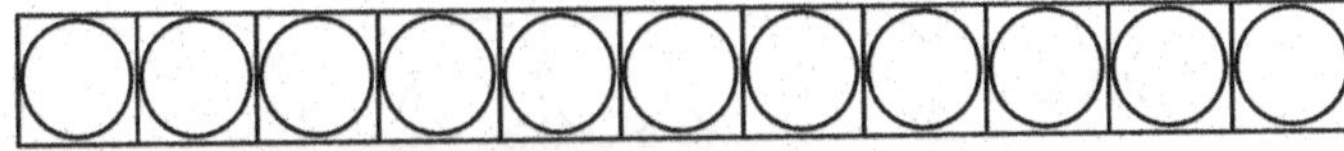

How to play: Complete the crossword puzzle by looking at the clues and unscrambling the answers. When the puzzle is complete, unscramble the circled letters to solve the BONUS.

JUMBLE® CROSSWORDS™

ACROSS

CLUE	ANSWER
1. Going to the bottom	NISGIKN
5. Release	TNEUI
6. Slow movement	ARCLW
7. Occupies	RSEEDIS

DOWN

CLUE	ANSWER
1. Sleep	RULBSME
2. Spots	TINCSEO
3. Home to Akranes	NAEICLD
4. Distorts	BSERAGL

CLUE: This actor turned down the male lead in *Ghost.*

BONUS 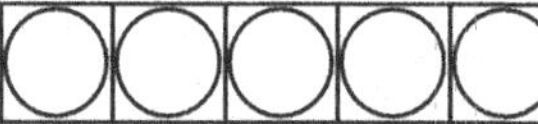 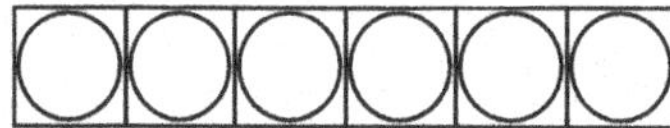

How to play: Complete the crossword puzzle by looking at the clues and unscrambling the answers. When the puzzle is complete, unscramble the circled letters to solve the BONUS.

JUMBLE® CROSSWORDS™

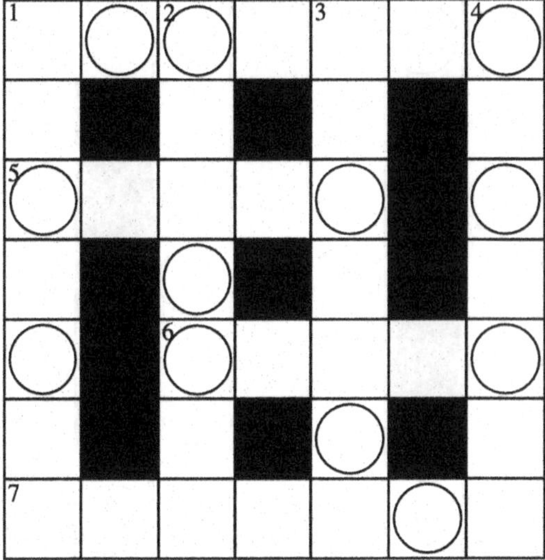

CLUE	ACROSS	ANSWER
1. Buyer		POHSREP
5. Large "body"		ECAON
6. Pharmaceuticals		RDSGU
7. Perpetual		TERELNA

CLUE	DOWN	ANSWER
1. Pestilence		UCSEROG
2. Outstanding		EVODREU
3. Short-legged swimmer		NIENUPG
4. Denial		ESARUFL

CLUE: As a way of honoring his work with the environment, this actor was asked to name a new breed of butterfly. He named it after his daughter, Georgia.

BONUS 

How to play: Complete the crossword puzzle by looking at the clues and unscrambling the answers. When the puzzle is complete, unscramble the circled letters to solve the BONUS.

JUMBLE CROSSWORDS™

ACROSS

CLUE	ANSWER
1. Fit	NTRTMUA
5. Cold ______	ECMAR
6. Camel relative	MAALL
7. Networks	TEYMSSS

DOWN

CLUE	ANSWER
1. Season ______	TCSTKIE
2. Pine ______	EDEELSN
3. Violent action	PMEARAG
4. Weekly seconds	NODMSYA

CLUE: This member of the Rock and Roll Hall of Fame was born in Newark, New Jersey, on October 13, 1941.

BONUS 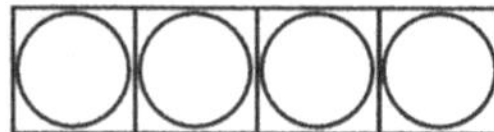 

How to play: Complete the crossword puzzle by looking at the clues and unscrambling the answers. When the puzzle is complete, unscramble the circled letters to solve the BONUS.

JUMBLE® CROSSWORDS™

ACROSS

CLUE	ANSWER
1. Top	EOBSLU
5. Terra-_____	ACTOT
6. Vitality	POMOH
7. Married	DEEWDD

DOWN

CLUE	ANSWER
1. Summon	BNCOKE
2. Result	UEOMOTC
3. Assembled together	RDSEAWM
4. Hurried	DREUHS

CLUE: The Environmental Protection Agency estimated that gas-powered ____ ____ contribute to about 5 percent of ozone pollution in the United States.

BONUS ◯◯◯◯ ◯◯◯◯◯◯

How to play: Complete the crossword puzzle by looking at the clues and unscrambling the answers. When the puzzle is complete, unscramble the circled letters to solve the BONUS.

JUMBLE® CROSSWORDS™

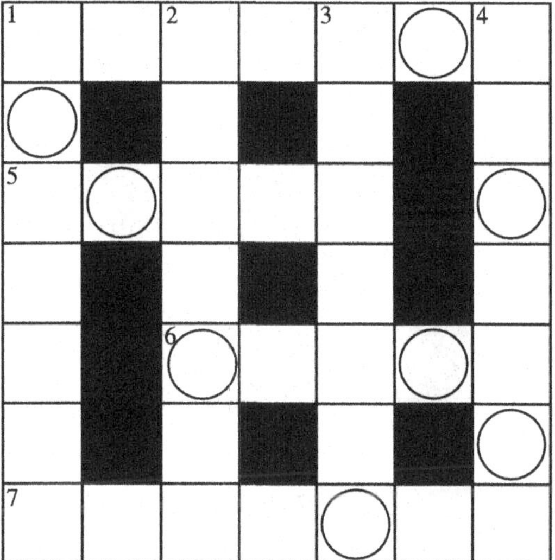

CLUE	ACROSS	ANSWER
1. Upper layer of dirt		PLOITOS
5. Black ______		HPESE
6. ______ aunt		TRGAE
7. Challenges		RISTESS

CLUE	DOWN	ANSWER
1. More savory		AERTIST
2. Promises		EDLGSEP
3. Treat unjustly		PORPSES
4. Distances		NELGHTS

CLUE: This is one of the largest ports in the world and home to more than 16 million people.

BONUS 

How to play Complete the crossword puzzle by looking at the clues and unscrambling the answers. When the puzzle is complete, unscramble the circled letters to solve the BONUS.

JUMBLE® CROSSWORDS™

ACROSS

CLUE	ANSWER
1. Parcel	AKGCEAP
5. Laugh _____	KRTCA
6. Ruminant mammal	ALMAL
7. Remainder	DERUSIE

DOWN

CLUE	ANSWER
1. Type of container	RTCIHEP
2. A white wine	HSAICLB
3. Clumsy	KWADAWR
4. Catch	NSEANRE

CLUE: You have millions of these in your body.

BONUS  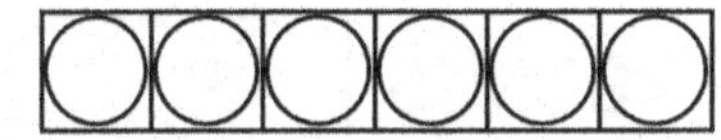

How to play: Complete the crossword puzzle by looking at the clues and unscrambling the answers. When the puzzle is complete, unscramble the circled letters to solve the BONUS.

JUMBLE® CROSSWORDS™

ACROSS

CLUE	ANSWER
1. Big ______	EPRSNED
5. Cements	ULGSE
6. Silly	NIEAN
7. Investigators	HELSTUS

DOWN

CLUE	ANSWER
1. Signs	LGIANSS
2. Evasive	EEVLISU
3. Withdrawn	DTIASTN
4. Hands over	RSEERDN

CLUE: This country is about the same size as South Dakota (about seventy-five thousand square miles).

BONUS 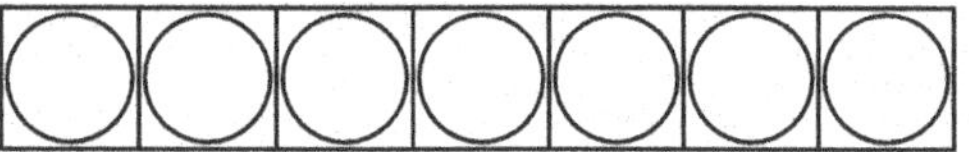

How to play: Complete the crossword puzzle by looking at the clues and unscrambling the answers. When the puzzle is complete, unscramble the circled letters to solve the BONUS.

ACROSS

CLUE	ANSWER
1. _____ tree	ROPACIT
5. Spacious	MOROY
6. Jacob or Dunne	RNIEE
7. Mythical flier	EUSPSAG

DOWN

CLUE	ANSWER
1. Type of vessel	RIAIHSP
2. Encouraging	NRGOIOT
3. Shyness	YCSOENS
4. Speeding _____	TISTCEK

CLUE: "I feel that today's puzzle is harder than yesterday's." D.L.H.

BONUS 

How to play — Complete the crossword puzzle by looking at the clues and unscrambling the answers. When the puzzle is complete, unscramble the circled letters to solve the BONUS.

JUMBLE® CROSSWORDS™

ACROSS

CLUE	ANSWER
1. A city	ASWRWA
5. Underground chambers	ECSVA
6. A description	RRLAU
7. A first name	DGLEAR

DOWN

CLUE	ANSWER
1. An adjective	EKIDCW
2. A gear	RRVSEEE
3. A country	UIAARST
4. A song	LBDAAL

CLUE: This puzzle's hints, for example

BONUS  

How to play: Complete the crossword puzzle by looking at the clues and unscrambling the answers. When the puzzle is complete, unscramble the circled letters to solve the BONUS.

JUMBLE® CROSSWORDS™

ACROSS CLUE	ANSWER
1. Straightened out	TSLTEDE
5. Tailor	PADTA
6. Home to Jacmel	AIHIT
7. Bashed	MALSDEM

DOWN CLUE	ANSWER
1. Sculpted forms	ATUTSSE
2. Cartilaginous tube	RAATEHC
3. ______ carbonate	TILIHMU
4. Soiled	DDIERIT

CLUE: This runs from east to west about 2,400 miles and from north to south about 2,000 miles.

BONUS 

How to play: Complete the crossword puzzle by looking at the clues and unscrambling the answers. When the puzzle is complete, unscramble the circled letters to solve the BONUS.

JUMBLE CROSSWORDS® Jamboree™

MASTER

PUZZLES

ACROSS

CLUE	ANSWER
1. Sea ______	PREESTN
5. Secures	LCSKO
6. The eighth of its kind	HEATT
7. Abilities	NTATLES

DOWN

CLUE	ANSWER
1. Seek	LTIOSIC
2. Dance ______	EAICLRT
3. ______ Europe	ARNEETS
4. Runways	RTMASCA

CLUE: More than 400 young men tried out for the lead roles on this sitcom.

BONUS

How to play: Complete the crossword puzzle by looking at the clues and unscrambling the answers. When the puzzle is complete, unscramble the circled letters to solve the BONUS.

ACROSS

CLUE	ANSWER
1. New beginning	TIERBHR
5. Joe or Frank	RAHYD
6. Circuits	POLSO
7. Steps	DSIRTES

DOWN

CLUE	ANSWER
1. Brings back	HERRISE
2. Cat ______	LAUGRRB
3. Lovable TV character	YARMNOD
4. Transporters, vehicles	RASHEES

CLUE: There are currently three of these in operation and based in three different regions of the United States.

BONUS 

How to play — Complete the crossword puzzle by looking at the clues and unscrambling the answers. When the puzzle is complete, unscramble the circled letters to solve the BONUS.

JUMBLE® CROSSWORDS™

ACROSS

CLUE	ANSWER
1. Poem parts	NTASAZS
5. ______ *Rae*	RONAM
6. Another time	NAIAG
7. Type of fighter	TAMDARO

DOWN

CLUE	ANSWER
1. Private place	NMUASTC
2. Up-to-date	BTRAASE
3. New ______	DAAZLEN
4. Conference	MESNIRA

CLUE: There are just four of these in the 48 contiguous United States.

BONUS 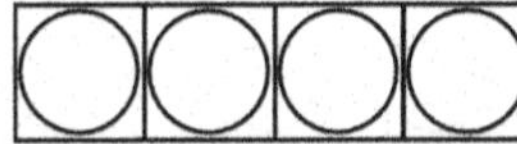 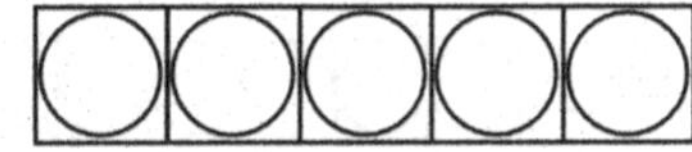

How to play: Complete the crossword puzzle by looking at the clues and unscrambling the answers. When the puzzle is complete, unscramble the circled letters to solve the BONUS.

JUMBLE® CROSSWORDS™

CLUE	ACROSS	ANSWER
1. Funny		MCICLAO
5. Interest _____		TRSEA
6. Lengths of cloth		ELSIV
7. Begrudges		NESTESR

CLUE	DOWN	ANSWER
1. Mail _____		RCIRREA
2. Reasons		TSVOEIM
3. _____ Sea		APICNAS
4. Migratory insects		UCLSSOT

CLUE: End

BONUS

How to play: Complete the crossword puzzle by looking at the clues and unscrambling the answers. When the puzzle is complete, unscramble the circled letters to solve the BONUS.

JUMBLE CROSSWORDS™

ACROSS

CLUE	ANSWER
1. Resisting control	ERTSEIV
5. Disordered state	HOASC
6. ______ gas	NIRET
7. Akin	LDERTEA

DOWN

CLUE	ANSWER
1. Bounce back	EOCVRRE
2. Springer ______	PLSAIEN
3. Examine	NIPETCS
4. Given off	MIETETD

CLUE: This woman said, "I know God will not give me anything I can't handle. I just wish that he didn't trust me so much."

BONUS  

How to play: Complete the crossword puzzle by looking at the clues and unscrambling the answers. When the puzzle is complete, unscramble the circled letters to solve the BONUS.

JUMBLE® CROSSWORDS™

CLUE	ACROSS	ANSWER
1. ______ point		EDLMICA
5. Earthen depression		AINBS
6. Picture		MGIEA
7. Ice cream dishes		NADESUS

CLUE	DOWN	ANSWER
1. Argues		BDASEET
2. ______ Gates		PSACNIA
3. Joe or one of 50		NMOAATN
4. Remains		LSIREGN

CLUE: The ______ ______ was established in 1945.

BONUS 

How to play: Complete the crossword puzzle by looking at the clues and unscrambling the answers. When the puzzle is complete, unscramble the circled letters to solve the BONUS.

JUMBLE® CROSSWORDS™

ACROSS

CLUE	ANSWER
1. Open	WUARPN
5. Vernacular	LGSAN
6. Coast	LDEGI
7. Manner	DHMTEO

DOWN

CLUE	ANSWER
1. Shaky	FNASEU
2. Argue	EGRNWAL
3. Sorrow	ASNUGIH
4. Rise	DCSNEA

CLUE: This cartoon figure debuted in 1852.

BONUS 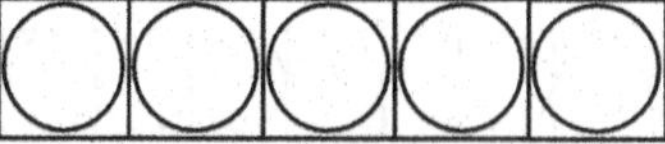 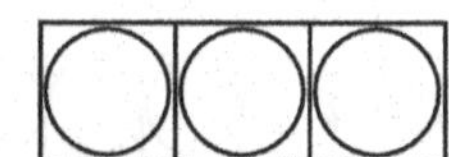

How to play: Complete the crossword puzzle by looking at the clues and unscrambling the answers. When the puzzle is complete, unscramble the circled letters to solve the BONUS.

ACROSS

CLUE	ANSWER
1. Being	SRONEP
5. Type of fastener	TIVRE
6. ______ song	NIERS
7. Come into contact with	OJNDIA

DOWN

CLUE	ANSWER
1. Saying	HESPAR
2. Changed	EIDRESV
3. North American region	ORITAON
4. Loose ______	NOCNNA

CLUE: A deltiologist collects these.

BONUS

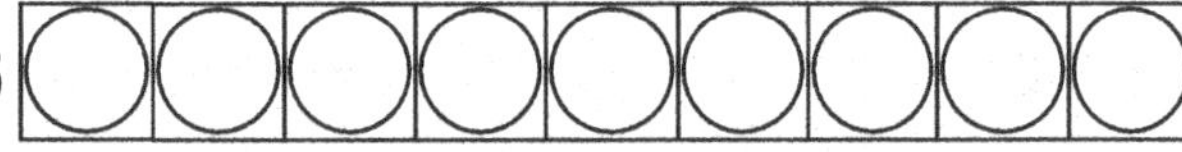

How to play: Complete the crossword puzzle by looking at the clues and unscrambling the answers. When the puzzle is complete, unscramble the circled letters to solve the BONUS.

ACROSS

CLUE	ANSWER
1. Began to be perceived	NDEAWD
5. European river	INRHE
6. Crew	PROTO
7. Withdraw	EDESCE

DOWN

CLUE	ANSWER
1. Compulsion by threat	RSEDUS
2. ______-blower	TISLHWE
3. Frightful sight	SEEOERY
4. Elementary	PSIELM

CLUE: This state is home to more than 8,500 lakes.

BONUS

How to play: Complete the crossword puzzle by looking at the clues and unscrambling the answers. When the puzzle is complete, unscramble the circled letters to solve the BONUS.

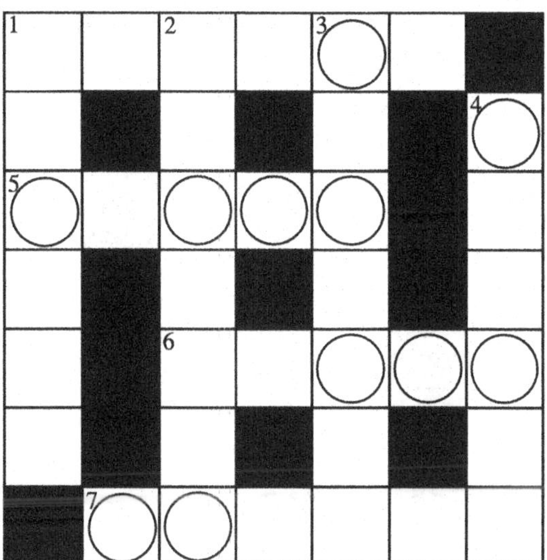

ACROSS

CLUE	ANSWER
1. Caught	DBENBA
5. Cypress _____	PWASM
6. Mel's sitcom business	NEIRD
7. Severe experience	ELDRAO

DOWN

CLUE	ANSWER
1. New Providence Island city	UASNAS
2. Sac	DELRDBA
3. Firmament	NEEASPX
4. *Dogs*, but not *dog*	LULRAP

CLUE: *McDonald's* and *Burger King*

BONUS  

How to play: Complete the crossword puzzle by looking at the clues and unscrambling the answers. When the puzzle is complete, unscramble the circled letters to solve the BONUS.

JUMBLE CROSSWORDS™

ACROSS

CLUE	ANSWER
1. Mixed up	LUDMEJB
5. Type of fabric	TIASN
6. Unmanned craft	NRODE
7. Reduces	KSSNIRH

DOWN

CLUE	ANSWER
1. Fools	RESJTES
2. Bullfighter	TAMDARO
3. A U.S. state capital	NILOCNL
4. Orders	EESDRCE

CLUE: This U.S. politician was born in 1936, in the Panama Canal Zone.

BONUS  

How to play: Complete the crossword puzzle by looking at the clues and unscrambling the answers. When the puzzle is complete, unscramble the circled letters to solve the BONUS.

ACROSS

CLUE	ANSWER
1. Crowded	MJDAEM
5. Provider	NDROO
6. Domain	AREML
7. Agitates	HSSEKA

DOWN

CLUE	ANSWER
1. Deduced	EUGDJD
2. ______ butterfly	AHNROMC
3. Designate	REAMKRA
4. Rises	LICSBM

CLUE: Some people are surprised to learn that this actor never won an Emmy.

BONUS 

How to play: Complete the crossword puzzle by looking at the clues and unscrambling the answers. When the puzzle is complete, unscramble the circled letters to solve the BONUS.

JUMBLE® CROSSWORDS™

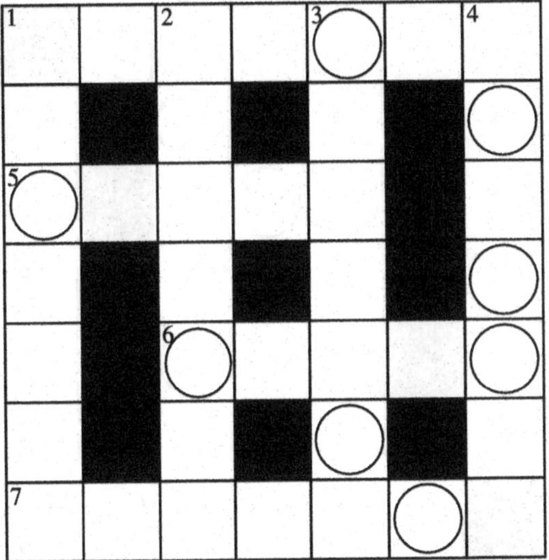

CLUE	ACROSS	ANSWER
1. Center		NSUCUEL
5. Grab		EZIES
6. A pouched mammal		AALOK
7. Genuine		RNIEECS

CLUE	DOWN	ANSWER
1. Snuggles comfortably		EENSLTS
2. ______ wire		HICCNEK
3. Raise		TVLAEEE
4. Cold ______		RGTSOEA

CLUE: There are more than 60 million ______ ______ books in print.

BONUS 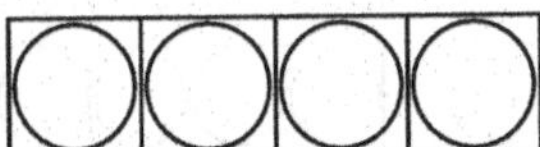 

How to play: Complete the crossword puzzle by looking at the clues and unscrambling the answers. When the puzzle is complete, unscramble the circled letters to solve the BONUS.

JUMBLE® CROSSWORDS™

ACROSS

CLUE	ANSWER
1. Confined	DILAEJ
5. Hate	AROHB
6. Kathy _____	TBSEA
7. Orders	ECDIST

DOWN

CLUE	ANSWER
1. _____ Cassidy	ANOJAN
2. Fictional Crane	BHACIDO
3. Wandering	RARTEIC
4. Whips	HWSSIK

CLUE: This actor, whose middle name is Joseph, was born on April 22, 1937, in New Jersey.

BONUS ◯◯◯◯ ◯◯◯◯◯◯◯◯◯

How to play: Complete the crossword puzzle by looking at the clues and unscrambling the answers. When the puzzle is complete, unscramble the circled letters to solve the BONUS.

JUMBLE® CROSSWORDS™

ACROSS

CLUE	ANSWER
1. Andrew _____	HNNOOJS
5. Pause indicator	MOCAM
6. Stomach lining	RIPET
7. Jagged	RCSGAYG

DOWN

CLUE	ANSWER
1. Riders	KCOSYEJ
2. Golden _____	MHTSREA
3. _____ power	AGSTYIN
4. _____ school	NEYRSRU

CLUE: This actor's first job as an entertainer was as a female dancer in a chorus line.

BONUS 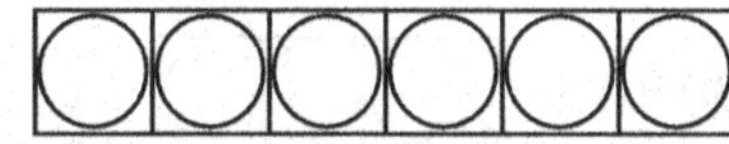

How to play: Complete the crossword puzzle by looking at the clues and unscrambling the answers. When the puzzle is complete, unscramble the circled letters to solve the BONUS.

JUMBLE® CROSSWORDS™

ACROSS

CLUE	ANSWER
1. Brash	TPIPYU
5. ______ squash	NORCA
6. Anxious	REEAG
7. Barbaric	BRAULT

DOWN

CLUE	ANSWER
1. Seven of nine	UAUSNR
2. Originator	RPEIEON
3. Later today	NOTIHTG
4. Keg	LRBEAR

CLUE: ______ debuted on store shelves in 1941.

BONUS 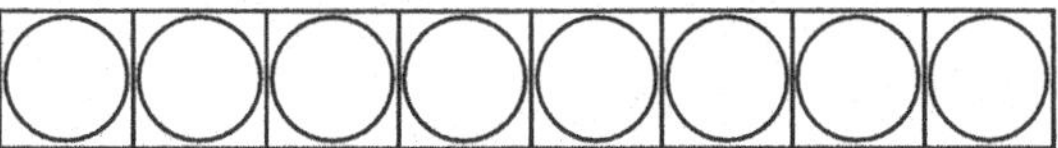

How to play: Complete the crossword puzzle by looking at the clues and unscrambling the answers. When the puzzle is complete, unscramble the circled letters to solve the BONUS.

JUMBLE® CROSSWORDS™

ACROSS

CLUE	ANSWER
1. Deadly	AELLHT
5. Special _____	TGSEU
6. Southern Indians	NSAIC
7. Consented	REDAEG

DOWN

CLUE	ANSWER
1. Pod, seed	EEMLGU
2. Overflowing	TGENIEM
3. Type of diplomat	AAEHTCT
4. Fresh	DEUNSU

CLUE: This actress is the only actress to win a Golden Globe, an Oscar,® and an Emmy in the same calendar year (as of 2004).

BONUS 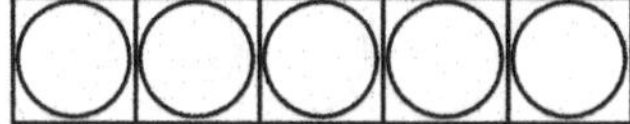 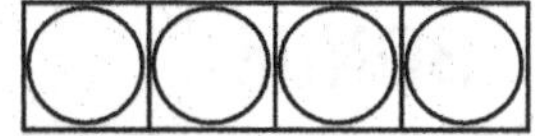

How to play — Complete the crossword puzzle by looking at the clues and unscrambling the answers. When the puzzle is complete, unscramble the circled letters to solve the BONUS.

JUMBLE® CROSSWORDS™

ACROSS

CLUE	ANSWER
1. Grown-up	TAUMER
5. Secure chamber	LVUTA
6. Type of string	NWTIE
7. To suppose	KROENC

DOWN

CLUE	ANSWER
1. Touching	NIOGVM
2. Administrator	TETRUSE
3. Consider again	KTERNIH
4. Natural chamber	NARVCE

CLUE: This man said, "I was trained to be an actor, not a star. I was trained to play roles, not to deal with fame and agents and lawyers and the press."

BONUS  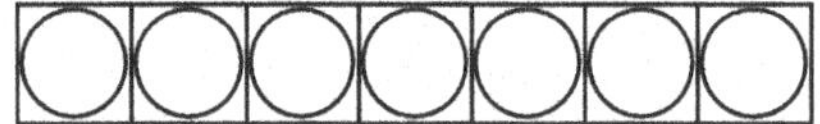

How to play: Complete the crossword puzzle by looking at the clues and unscrambling the answers. When the puzzle is complete, unscramble the circled letters to solve the BONUS.

JUMBLE® CROSSWORDS™

ACROSS

CLUE	ANSWER
1. Capital	ETSSSA
5. Room	PCEAS
6. Stuff	ROGEG
7. Harry _____	NARTMU

DOWN

CLUE	ANSWER
1. Transfer	ASISNG
2. Self-assured walk	WERSGGA
3. Proposed truth	TEHMROE
4. Block	EENRSC

CLUE: _____, _____, is home to approximately 3 million people. It was conquered in the 1450s by the Ottoman Turks, who held it for almost four centuries.

BONUS ○○○○○○, ○○○○○○

How to play Complete the crossword puzzle by looking at the clues and unscrambling the answers. When the puzzle is complete, unscramble the circled letters to solve the BONUS.

JUMBLE® CROSSWORDS™

ACROSS

CLUE	ANSWER
1. Reduced calorie intake	DITDEE
5. Straight up	ETSPE
6. A U.S. city	HMAAO
7. _____ oil	NPETUA

DOWN

CLUE	ANSWER
1. Disappointment	DSIYAM
2. Unattractive sight	ESEYREO
3. Clarify	NEIXAPL
4. Oddity	TMTUAN

CLUE: Scholars believe that this nursery rhyme is more than 500 years old.

BONUS  

How to play: Complete the crossword puzzle by looking at the clues and unscrambling the answers. When the puzzle is complete, unscramble the circled letters to solve the BONUS.

JUMBLE® CROSSWORDS™

ACROSS

CLUE	ANSWER
1. Pierce, stab	RSEKWE
5. Spacious	LAMEP
6. Slick	ELEKS
7. Copy _____	TIDROE

DOWN

CLUE	ANSWER
1. Saved	APSDER
2. Revealed	POXSEDE
3. Part	LENTEEM
4. Sponsor	RBEAKC

CLUE: This man was the only network anchor present at the collapse of the Berlin Wall in 1989.

BONUS 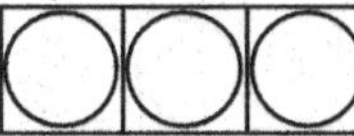 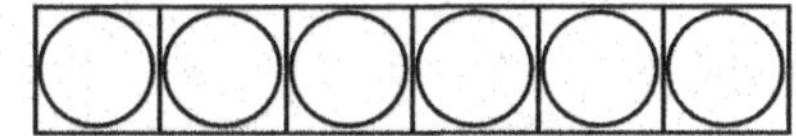

How to play: Complete the crossword puzzle by looking at the clues and unscrambling the answers. When the puzzle is complete, unscramble the circled letters to solve the BONUS.

JUMBLE® CROSSWORDS™

ACROSS

CLUE	ANSWER
1. Type of rock	TREEOM
5. A style of music	ULSBE
6. Power	RFECO
7. Show designation	PETERA

DOWN

CLUE	ANSWER
1. Packed	EBODMB
2. Ascomycetous fungi	FLTUEFR
3. See	BRSOEEV
4. Warning	AVCTEA

CLUE: _____ rank as one of the safest forms of transportation, with only one fatality every 100 million miles traveled.

BONUS 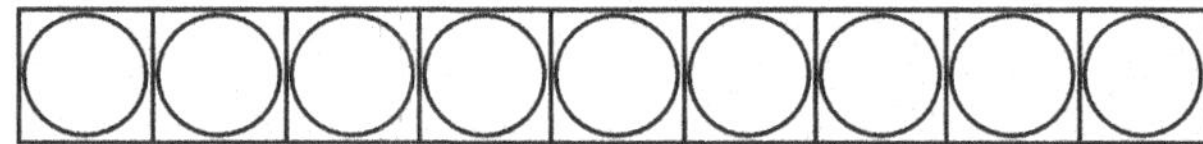

How to play: Complete the crossword puzzle by looking at the clues and unscrambling the answers. When the puzzle is complete, unscramble the circled letters to solve the BONUS.

ACROSS

CLUE	ANSWER
1. Show	PEDITC
5. A synthetic fabric	YOARN
6. Mistake	RERRO
7. Swiped	TSELON

DOWN

CLUE	ANSWER
1. ______ deposit	RTIDCE
2. ______ plan	ANTPEYM
3. Govern	LNOCRTO
4. Small unit	MNIORC

CLUE: The first known ______ date back to ancient Greece.

BONUS

How to play: Complete the crossword puzzle by looking at the clues and unscrambling the answers. When the puzzle is complete, unscramble the circled letters to solve the BONUS.

JUMBLE® CROSSWORDS™

ACROSS

CLUE	ANSWER
1. Odd	RCSWYE
5. ______ Prize	BONLE
6. Chariot ______	ASECR
7. Meter	MRHHYT

DOWN

CLUE	ANSWER
1. Rationally	NSALEY
2. New beginning	BIHRTRE
3. Type of feline	LIWCDTA
4. Resinous substance	ASABML

CLUE: Construction on the ______ ______ began in 1961.

BONUS 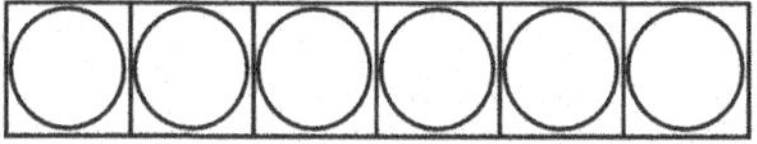 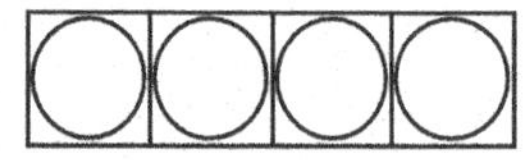

How to play: Complete the crossword puzzle by looking at the clues and unscrambling the answers. When the puzzle is complete, unscramble the circled letters to solve the BONUS.

ACROSS

CLUE	ANSWER
1. See	LHBEDO
5. Rotating blade	TRROO
6. Austrian doctor	DRFUE
7. Hot _____	TALEPS

DOWN

CLUE	ANSWER
1. Bivalent metal	RBMIUA
2. Mean	LTHAEFU
3. Jupiter, to the rest	RATLEGS
4. Giant _____	NPSAAD

CLUE: As recently as the thirties, _____ injections were commonly used by physicians to treat alcoholism.

BONUS 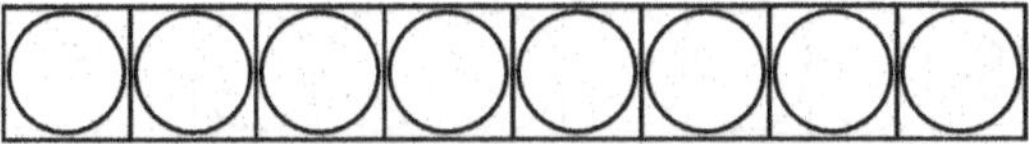

How to play: Complete the crossword puzzle by looking at the clues and unscrambling the answers. When the puzzle is complete, unscramble the circled letters to solve the BONUS.

#153

JUMBLE® CROSSWORDS™

ACROSS

CLUE	ANSWER
1. Piercing	LHLSIR
5. Cut	DMWOE
6. ______ coffee	RISIH
7. Distance	HNLTGE

DOWN

CLUE	ANSWER
1. Top	MUSTIM
2. C.E. TV show	WRIHEDA
3. Place to sleep	DGGLION
4. August, for example	HGETIH

CLUE: The ______ and its landscaped grounds occupy 18 acres of ground.

BONUS 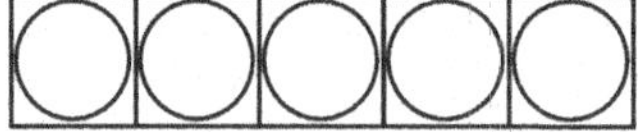 

How to play: Complete the crossword puzzle by looking at the clues and unscrambling the answers. When the puzzle is complete, unscramble the circled letters to solve the BONUS.

JUMBLE CROSSWORDS™

ACROSS

CLUE	ANSWER
1. Carnivorous African animal	AJCLKA
5. Extent	ERGNA
6. Facial expression	LSWOC
7. Composition	KAUEPM

DOWN

CLUE	ANSWER
1. Football shirt	RJSEYE
2. A card game	ANTACAS
3. Extraordinary	MWOSAEE
4. Beat	LAWPOL

CLUE: _____, _____, lies on the Kanto plain. It's intersected by the Sumida River and has an extensive network of canals.

BONUS 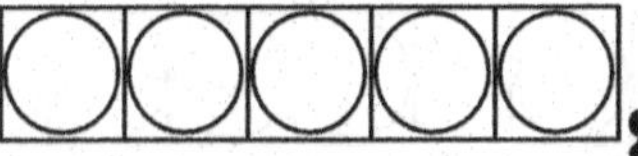, 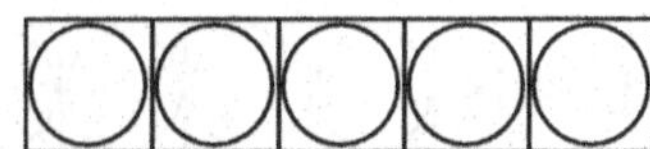

How to play: Complete the crossword puzzle by looking at the clues and unscrambling the answers. When the puzzle is complete, unscramble the circled letters to solve the BONUS.

CLUE	ACROSS	ANSWER
1. Largest		TBSIEGG
5. Garden herbs		ESKEL
6. Barrier		NEECF
7. Soothe		LEIEREV

CLUE	DOWN	ANSWER
1. Support		TLBSROE
2. Merry		LELGFEU
3. Central meaning		ESESECN
4. ______ artist		PARTEEZ

CLUE: Approximately 95 percent of all the Earth's animal species are ______.

BONUS

How to play: Complete the crossword puzzle by looking at the clues and unscrambling the answers. When the puzzle is complete, unscramble the circled letters to solve the BONUS.

JUMBLE® CROSSWORDS™

ACROSS

CLUE	ANSWER
1. ______ sofa	RPESELE
5. ______-cut	ELCNA
6. Baker or Bryant	TNIAA
7. Pierces	KWRSSEE

DOWN

CLUE	ANSWER
1. Portions	RESSOTC
2. Lift	LVETAEE
3. Contemplative	NEVPIES
4. Baggage porters	DERACSP

CLUE: In the United States, the standard width between ______ ______ is 4 feet, 8½ inches.

BONUS

How to play: Complete the crossword puzzle by looking at the clues and unscrambling the answers. When the puzzle is complete, unscramble the circled letters to solve the BONUS.

JUMBLE® CROSSWORDS™

ACROSS

CLUE	ANSWER
1. Sorcerous	ACALMIG
5. Prepare	RMOGO
6. Complain	PGRIE
7. Ice _____	TKSRESA

DOWN

CLUE	ANSWER
1. Field _____	TASMENG
2. Home to Athens	EGIGROA
3. Accumulate	MOCIPEL
4. Minds	NISLETS

CLUE: This movie won Oscars® for Best Picture, Best Actor, Best Director, and Best Original Screenplay.

BONUS 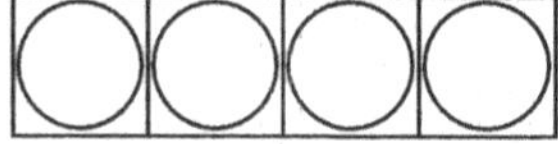 

How to play: Complete the crossword puzzle by looking at the clues and unscrambling the answers. When the puzzle is complete, unscramble the circled letters to solve the BONUS.

JUMBLE® CROSSWORDS™

ACROSS

CLUE	ANSWER
1. Hamilton, to Bermuda	PCTILAA
5. Harass	UDHNO
6. _____ Spiner	RTBNE
7. Type of cloud	TSATSUR

DOWN

CLUE	ANSWER
1. Colleagues	HOCROST
2. Type of installer, repairman	RULBMEP
3. Neatest	DITEITS
4. Finds	LASEOTC

CLUE: The average adult _____ _____ weighs from 2.25 pounds to 3.25 pounds.

BONUS 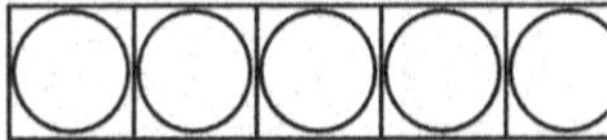 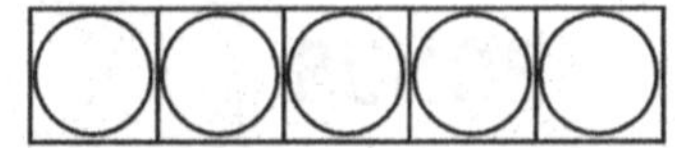

How to play: Complete the crossword puzzle by looking at the clues and unscrambling the answers. When the puzzle is complete, unscramble the circled letters to solve the BONUS.

ACROSS

CLUE	ANSWER
1. Shrivels	TIEHRSW
5. Separated	RPTAA
6. Fipple _____	ULFET
7. Stimulates	XEICSET

DOWN

CLUE	ANSWER
1. Squabble	RGAWNEL
2. _____ light	FICFRTA
3. Confide in	TNEURTS
4. Rents from a renter	BSUELTS

CLUE: Certain

BONUS

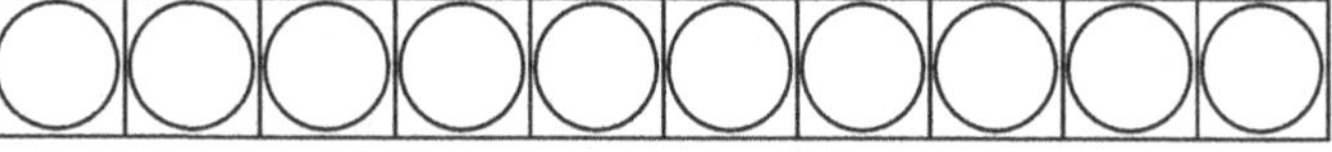

How to play: Complete the crossword puzzle by looking at the clues and unscrambling the answers. When the puzzle is complete, unscramble the circled letters to solve the BONUS.

JUMBLE® CROSSWORDS™

ACROSS

CLUE	ANSWER
1. Socks, stocking, etc.	HYROEIS
5. Time ______	MTPSA
6. Ooze out	UDXEE
7. Ceaseless	DSNEELS

DOWN

CLUE	ANSWER
1. Caring program	EHCOIPS
2. Type of plant	DAEEWES
3. Adopt	PEUEOSS
4. NYC players	NEAYSKE

CLUE: ______ ______ service began in 1860.

BONUS  

How to play: Complete the crossword puzzle by looking at the clues and unscrambling the answers. When the puzzle is complete, unscramble the circled letters to solve the BONUS.

JUMBLE CROSSWORDS® Jamboree™

DOUBLE BONUS

PUZZLES

ACROSS

CLUE	ANSWER
1. _____ board	RAOELP
5. Formal charge	UAACCSL
6. Type of scientist	MEHSITC
7. Puts on	TGESSA

DOWN

CLUE	ANSWER
1. Type of walk	ARPCEN
2. B.G. for example	EHCSITR
3. Durable	LGNAIST
4. Schedules	ASSETL

How to play—Complete the crossword puzzle by looking at the clues and unscrambling the answers. When the puzzle is complete, unscramble the circled letters to solve the BONUS.

DOUBLE BONUS

The circled letters can be unscrambled to form two different BONUS answers.

CLUE: Protects

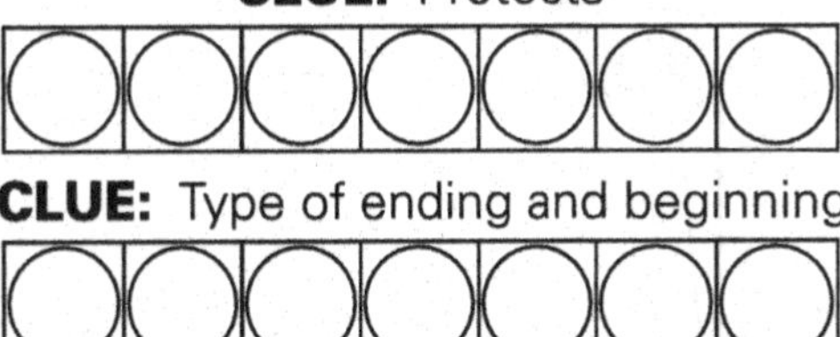

CLUE: Type of ending and beginning

I would love to hear from you . . .
You can e-mail me at:
DLHoyt@aol.com

ACROSS

CLUE	ANSWER
1. _____ vow	NLSMEO
5. Aromatic substance	ENICNES
6. Comfort	LOCESON
7. Repulses	RSELEP

DOWN

CLUE	ANSWER
1. Bait's partner	HWCSIT
2. Poetic _____	NIESECL
3. _____ cover	AMOHELN
4. Measuring devices	EMSTRE

How to play—Complete the crossword puzzle by looking at the clues and unscrambling the answers. When the puzzle is complete, unscramble the circled letters to solve the BONUS.

DOUBLE BONUS

The circled letters can be unscrambled to form two different BONUS answers.

CLUE: Automotive pioneer Ferdinand _____

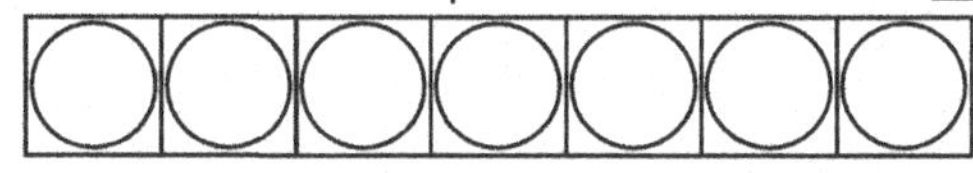

CLUE: Attached structures

I would love to hear from you . . .
You can e-mail me at:
DLHoyt@aol.com

ACROSS

CLUE	ANSWER
1. Rosy	PATUEB
5. Asphalt _____	HNLIGSE
6. Type of tire	TERERDA
7. _____ Moyet	LASINO

DOWN

CLUE	ANSWER
1. Not decided	RNSEUU
2. English city	RBITSLO
3. African city	LGEISRA
4. Tough tissue	NOTNDE

How to play—Complete the crossword puzzle by looking at the clues and unscrambling the answers. When the puzzle is complete, unscramble the circled letters to solve the BONUS.

DOUBLE BONUS

The circled letters can be unscrambled to form two different BONUS answers.

CLUE: _____ loan

CLUE: Underdeveloped

I would love to hear from you . . .
You can e-mail me at:
DLHoyt@aol.com

PUZZLE
#164

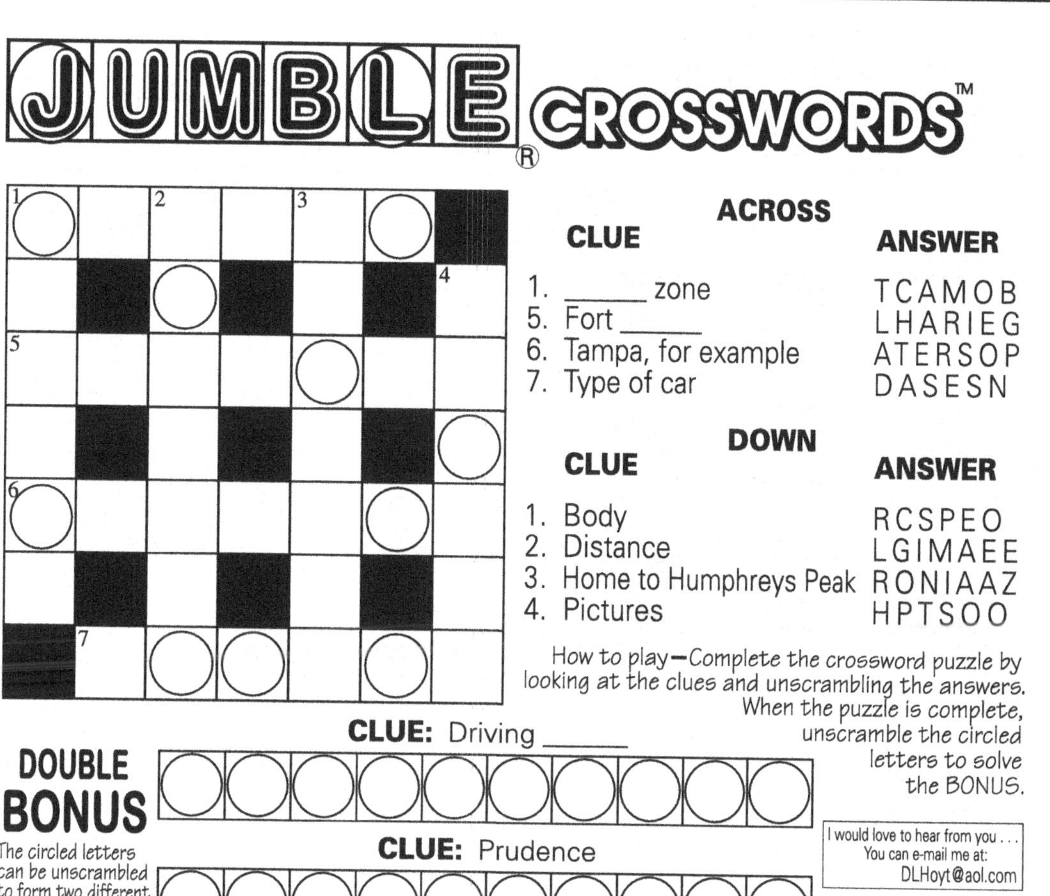
JUMBLE CROSSWORDS™
1
2
3
4
5
6
7
ACROSS
CLUE
ANSWER
1. ______ zone
TCAMOB
5. Fort ______
LHARIEG
6. Tampa, for example
ATERSOP
7. Type of car
DASESN
DOWN
CLUE
ANSWER
1. Body
RCSPEO
2. Distance
LGIMAEE
3. Home to Humphreys Peak
RONIAAZ
4. Pictures
HPTSOO
How to play—Complete the crossword puzzle by looking at the clues and unscrambling the answers. When the puzzle is complete, unscramble the circled letters to solve the BONUS.
CLUE: Driving ______
DOUBLE BONUS
The circled letters can be unscrambled to form two different BONUS answers.
CLUE: Prudence
I would love to hear from you . . . You can e-mail me at: DLHoyt@aol.com

ACROSS

CLUE	ANSWER
1. Cherry _____	RUALLE
5. High _____	ERTSAON
6. Extra	LRSUSPU
7. Called	HEOPDN

DOWN

CLUE	ANSWER
1. Most recent	TLSETA
2. Discover	HUTNREA
3. The fifth of its kind	NIPSELO
4. Fresh, unsoiled	DUSNEU

How to play—Complete the crossword puzzle by looking at the clues and unscrambling the answers. When the puzzle is complete, unscramble the circled letters to solve the BONUS.

DOUBLE BONUS

The circled letters can be unscrambled to form two different BONUS answers.

CLUE: 1986 movie

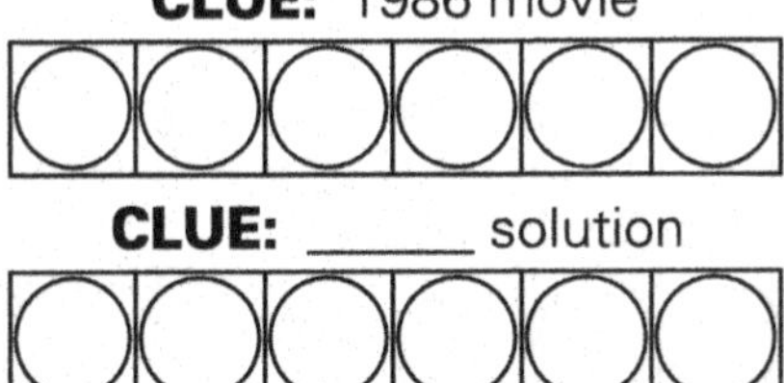

CLUE: _____ solution

I would love to hear from you . . .
You can e-mail me at:
DLHoyt@aol.com

ACROSS

CLUE	ANSWER
1. Cornered	NGEADL
5. Rare	LANSUUU
6. Roving	DMCOINA
7. Reserved	TEDSRO

DOWN

CLUE	ANSWER
1. Former students	MULINA
2. ______ chef	UOGMRTE
3. Home to Riobamba	DAUOECR
4. Cut	LSCIDE

How to play—Complete the crossword puzzle by looking at the clues and unscrambling the answers. When the puzzle is complete, unscramble the circled letters to solve the BONUS.

DOUBLE BONUS

The circled letters can be unscrambled to form two different BONUS answers.

CLUE: Warmer

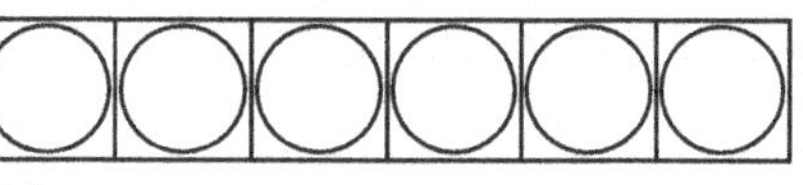

CLUE: Singer/actress born in New Jersey

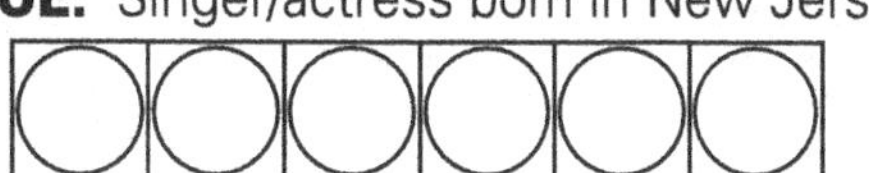

I would love to hear from you . . .
You can e-mail me at:
DLHoyt@aol.com

PUZZLE
#167

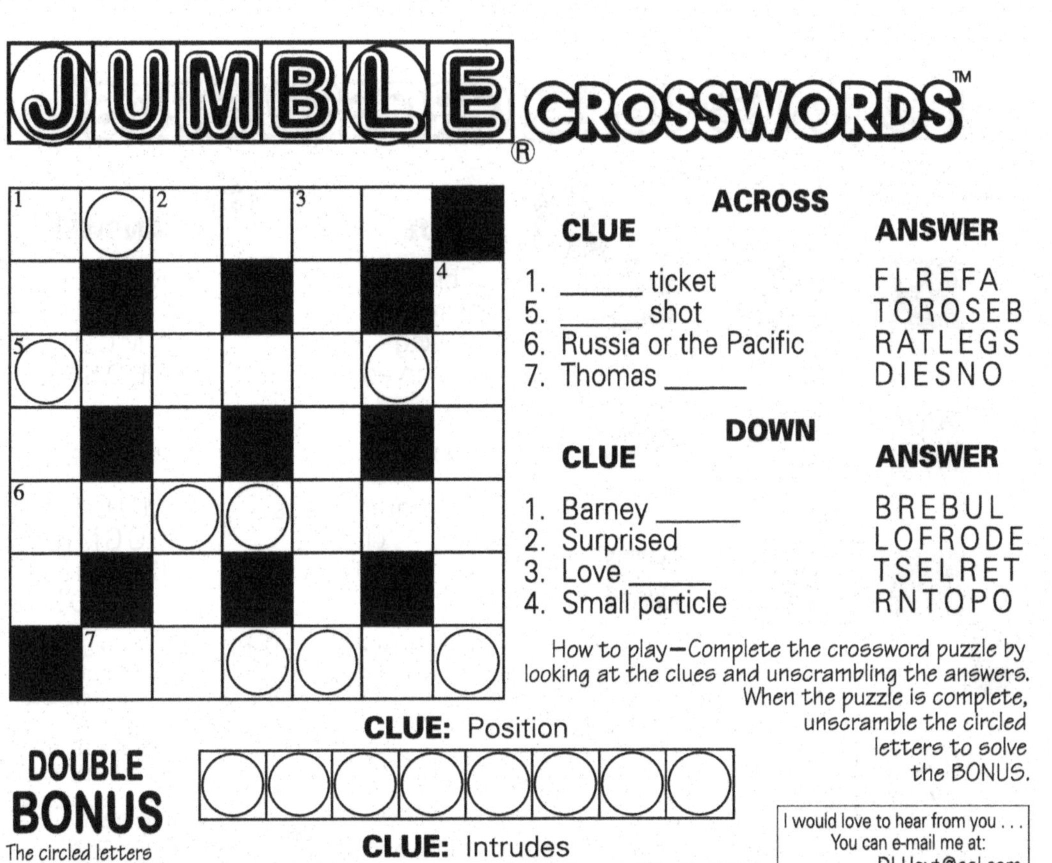

JUMBLE CROSSWORDS™
ACROSS
CLUE ANSWER
1. ______ ticket FLREFA
5. ______ shot TOROSEB
6. Russia or the Pacific RATLEGS
7. Thomas ______ DIESNO
DOWN
CLUE ANSWER
1. Barney ______ BREBUL
2. Surprised LOFRODE
3. Love ______ TSELRET
4. Small particle RNTOPO
How to play—Complete the crossword puzzle by looking at the clues and unscrambling the answers. When the puzzle is complete, unscramble the circled letters to solve the BONUS.
CLUE: Position
DOUBLE BONUS
The circled letters can be unscrambled to form two different BONUS answers.
CLUE: Intrudes
I would love to hear from you . . . You can e-mail me at: DLHoyt@aol.com

ACROSS

CLUE	ANSWER
1. Cool	HLICYL
5. Embolden	NSPIEIR
6. Carry out	XEEUCET
7. Jet _____	RETSMA

DOWN

CLUE	ANSWER
1. Wound up	LIOCDE
2. Examine	NSIEPTC
3. _____ suit	ELSIREU
4. Turn in	DREMEE

How to play—Complete the crossword puzzle by looking at the clues and unscrambling the answers. When the puzzle is complete, unscramble the circled letters to solve the BONUS.

DOUBLE BONUS

The circled letters can be unscrambled to form two different BONUS answers.

CLUE: Inconvenient

CLUE: Insignificant

I would love to hear from you . . .
You can e-mail me at:
DLHoyt@aol.com

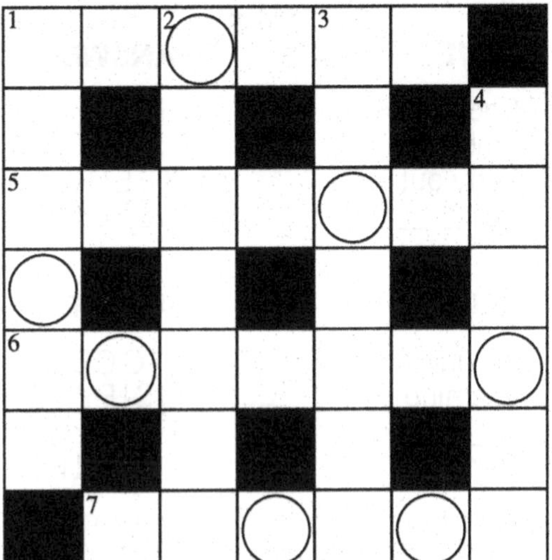

ACROSS

CLUE	ANSWER
1. Conclude	EEUDDC
5. Home to Burgenland	TAARUIS
6. Installment	PIOEESD
7. ______ pass	NAESOS

DOWN

CLUE	ANSWER
1. Car ______	EDRELA
2. Scorn	PIESEDS
3. Investigative	RUCISUO
4. Type of chamber	AREVNC

How to play—Complete the crossword puzzle by looking at the clues and unscrambling the answers. When the puzzle is complete, unscramble the circled letters to solve the BONUS.

DOUBLE BONUS

The circled letters can be unscrambled to form two different BONUS answers.

CLUE: Released

CLUE: Snow _____ or ______ moth

I would love to hear from you . . .
You can e-mail me at:
DLHoyt@aol.com

JUMBLE® CROSSWORDS™

ACROSS

CLUE	ANSWER
1. Movie _____	EEWRIV
5. Sea _____	NPEESTR
6. Going away	TIGXIEN
7. Evades	DDEOSG

DOWN

CLUE	ANSWER
1. Hustled	HUEDRS
2. 1958 J.S. movie	TGIREOV
3. _____ dress	EGENVIN
4. Puts on	ATEGSS

How to play—Complete the crossword puzzle by looking at the clues and unscrambling the answers. When the puzzle is complete, unscramble the circled letters to solve the BONUS.

DOUBLE BONUS

The circled letters can be unscrambled to form two different BONUS answers.

CLUE: Harsh

CLUE: Actor born in 1964

I would love to hear from you . . .
You can e-mail me at:
DLHoyt@aol.com

ACROSS

CLUE	ANSWER
1. Gloomy	LDIAMS
5. String	ENTWI
6. Laughable	LROLD
7. Return	TVRREE

DOWN

CLUE	ANSWER
1. Going out	TDGNIA
2. Cheat	NWISELD
3. Fantastic	EWMOSEA
4. Small hole	YEEETL

How to play—Complete the crossword puzzle by looking at the clues and unscrambling the answers. When the puzzle is complete, unscramble the circled letters to solve the BONUS.

DOUBLE BONUS

The circled letters can be unscrambled to form two different BONUS answers.

CLUE: Angrily

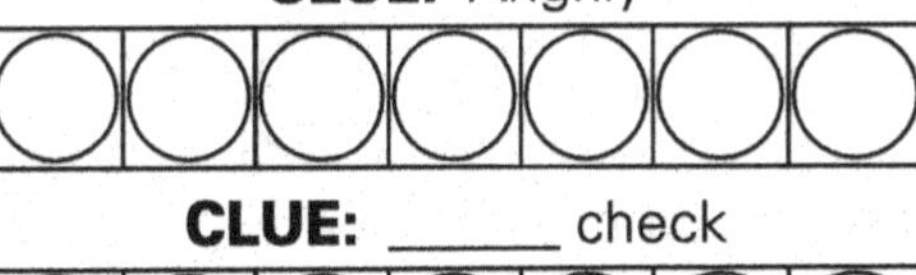

CLUE: ______ check

I would love to hear from you . . .
You can e-mail me at:
DLHoyt@aol.com

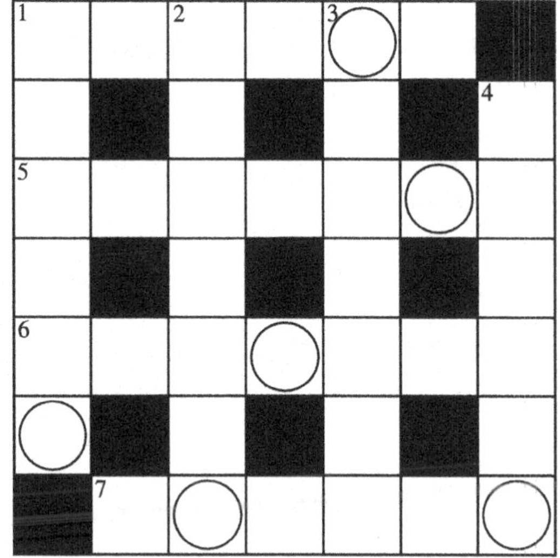

ACROSS

CLUE	ANSWER
1. Break	THASIU
5. Sharp _____	DEDHRAC
6. Study	AXIMEEN
7. Blends	RGSMEE

DOWN

CLUE	ANSWER
1. Cut	KAHCDE
2. Batting _____	EAGVRAE
3. Eternal	NNDUIYG
4. Course areas	REGSNE

How to play—Complete the crossword puzzle by looking at the clues and unscrambling the answers. When the puzzle is complete, unscramble the circled letters to solve the BONUS.

DOUBLE BONUS

The circled letters can be unscrambled to form two different BONUS answers.

CLUE: A mythical female

CLUE: Entertained

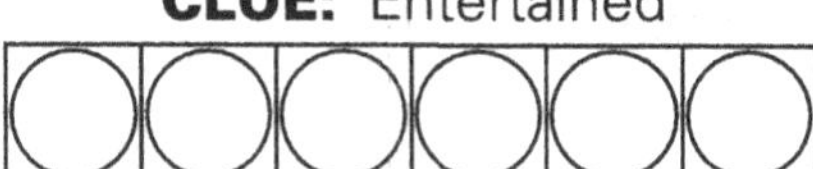

I would love to hear from you . . .
You can e-mail me at:
DLHoyt@aol.com

ACROSS

CLUE	ANSWER
1. Distributed	USESID
5. Express an opinion	PEOIN
6. French artist	EAGSD
7. Connective tissue	NTOEDN

DOWN

CLUE	ANSWER
1. Sardonic	NOIRIC
2. Cheat	WISELDN
3. Appeared	EGDEMRE
4. Picked	HSECNO

How to play—Complete the crossword puzzle by looking at the clues and unscrambling the answers. When the puzzle is complete, unscramble the circled letters to solve the BONUS.

DOUBLE BONUS

The circled letters can be unscrambled to form two different BONUS answers.

CLUE: Together

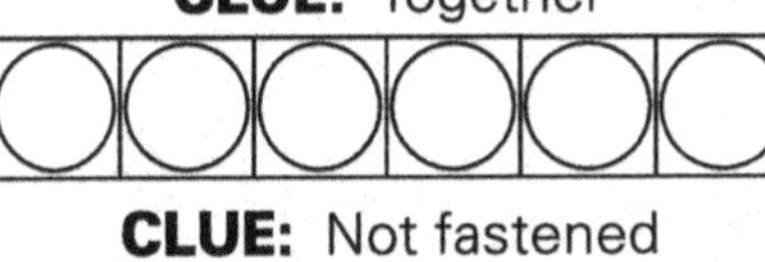

CLUE: Not fastened

I would love to hear from you . . . You can e-mail me at: DLHoyt@aol.com

JUMBLE CROSSWORDS® Jamboree™

TRIPLE BONUS PUZZLES

ACROSS

CLUE	ANSWER
1. Method	ANEMRN
5. Hindered	TTNUSDE
6. Movable arrow	PINENSR
7. Sloping channels	TUEHSC

DOWN

CLUE	ANSWER
1. Mistreat	EMSIUS
2. Feed	UHONIRS
3. Dead	TCXENIT
4. Beautifies	DAROSN

How to play - Complete the crossword puzzle by looking at the clues and unscrambling the answers. When the puzzle is complete, unscramble the circled letters to solve the BONUS.

CLUE: A tennis player's first name

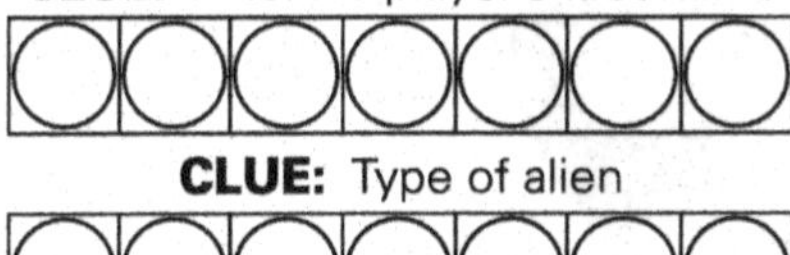

TRIPLE BONUS

The circled letters can be unscrambled to form three different BONUS answers.

CLUE: Type of alien

CLUE: Type of monkey

I would love to hear from you . . .
You can e-mail me at:
DLHoyt@aol.com

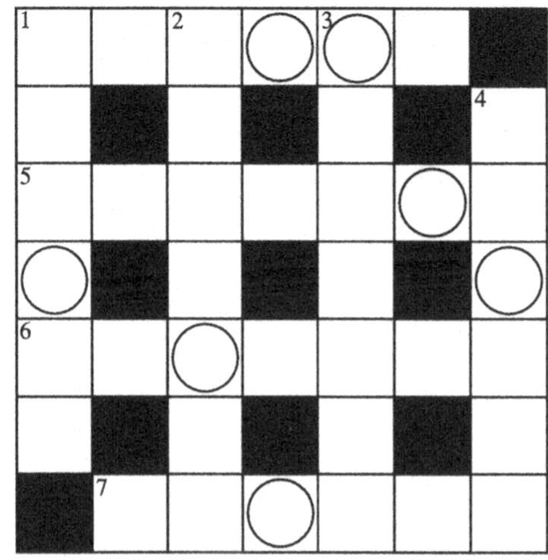

ACROSS

CLUE	ANSWER
1. Body	PSOECR
5. Wandered	MRLBDEA
6. Unyielding	DTANAAM
7. Go to	NTETDA

DOWN

CLUE	ANSWER
1. Gather	RCLAOR
2. Unused piece	TMERANN
3. Save	LGAAESV
4. Changed	DTDEIE

How to play—Complete the crossword puzzle by looking at the clues and unscrambling the answers. When the puzzle is complete, unscramble the circled letters to solve the BONUS.

CLUE: Birthday ______

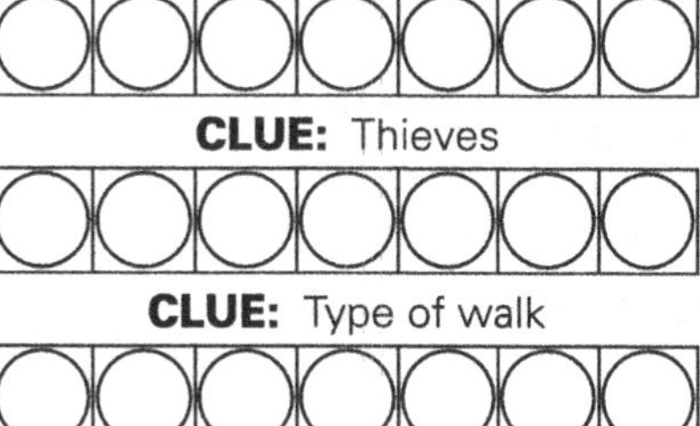

CLUE: Thieves

CLUE: Type of walk

TRIPLE BONUS

The circled letters can be unscrambled to form three different BONUS answers.

I would love to hear from you . . .
You can e-mail me at:
DLHoyt@aol.com

ACROSS

CLUE	ANSWER
1. An earth color	NIESAN
5. Avoided	RVEADET
6. Easier to understand	AEELRCR
7. Delays	LATSSL

DOWN

CLUE	ANSWER
1. ______ party	AESHCR
2. Trace ______	LEEEMTN
3. ______ resource	RTLANUA
4. Reveres	DAROSE

How to play—Complete the crossword puzzle by looking at the clues and unscrambling the answers. When the puzzle is complete, unscramble the circled letters to solve the BONUS.

TRIPLE BONUS

The circled letters can be unscrambled to form three different BONUS answers.

CLUE: Re-educate

CLUE: A piece of land

CLUE: Type of instructor

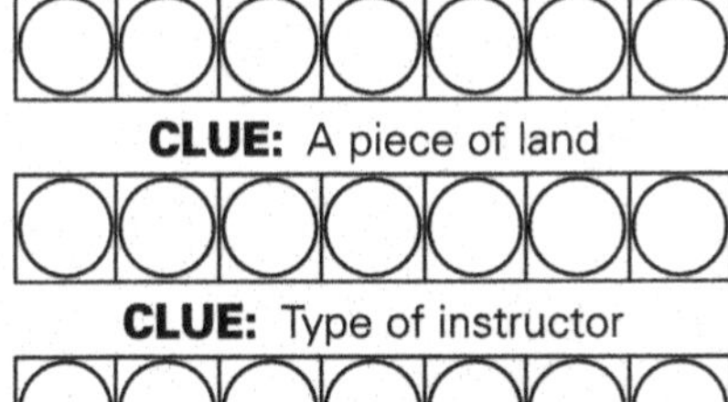

I would love to hear from you . . .
You can e-mail me at:
DLHoyt@aol.com

JUMBLE CROSSWORDS™

ACROSS

CLUE	ANSWER
1. Planned	DSETAL
5. Green _____	KNAES
6. Recurring beat	TCISU
7. _____ level	NYGEER

DOWN

CLUE	ANSWER
1. Operating _____	YSSMET
2. Type of horse	RAAIBNA
3. _____ set	EECRRTO
4. Shiny	LSOGYS

How to play—Complete the crossword puzzle by looking at the clues and unscrambling the answers. When the puzzle is complete, unscramble the circled letters to solve the BONUS.

TRIPLE BONUS

The circled letters can be unscrambled to form three different BONUS answers.

CLUE: Early road builders

◯◯◯◯◯◯

CLUE: Lordly dwellings

◯◯◯◯◯◯

CLUE: 1996 M.G. movie

◯◯◯◯◯◯

I would love to hear from you . . .
You can e-mail me at:
DLHoyt@aol.com

JUMBLE® CROSSWORDS™

ACROSS

CLUE	ANSWER
1. Dormant	TTNALE
5. Copy	CIMMI
6. Overturn	EUPTS
7. Type of shelter, structure	BAAACN

DOWN

CLUE	ANSWER
1. Flexible	BLMIER
2. Type of fried food	MAETUPR
3. Mediterranean city	AICINSO
4. ______ Christie	TAAAHG

How to play—Complete the crossword puzzle by looking at the clues and unscrambling the answers. When the puzzle is complete, unscramble the circled letters to solve the BONUS.

CLUE: Important building

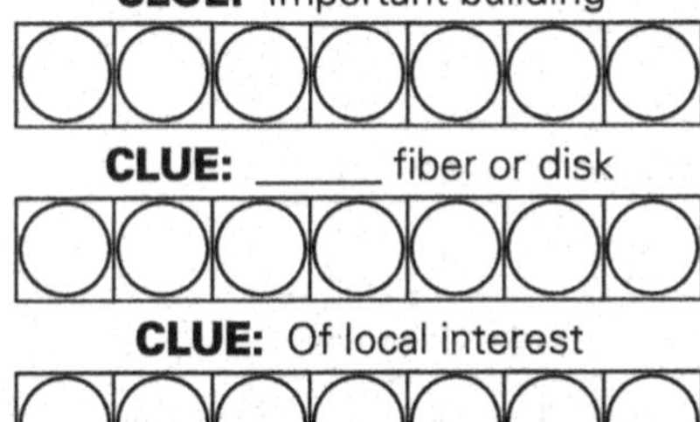

CLUE: ______ fiber or disk

CLUE: Of local interest

TRIPLE BONUS

The circled letters can be unscrambled to form three different BONUS answers.

I would love to hear from you . . .
You can e-mail me at:
DLHoyt@aol.com

ANSWERS

1. **Answers:**
   1A—CLICHÉ 5A—FRIED 6A—IVORY 7A—SLATED
   1D—COFFIN 2D—INITIAL 3D—HIDEOUT 4D—PLAYED
   Bonus: The size of the first ____ on the moon was about 13 inches long—FOOTPRINT
2. **Answers:**
   1A—MAYHEM 5A—PERTH 6A—ASCOT 7A—WEALTH
   1D—MAPLES 2D—YARDAGE 3D—ETHICAL 4D—SKETCH
   Bonus: Early Spanish sailors called this site *Cayo Hueso* (Bone Island)—KEY WEST
3. **Answers:**
   1A—TOMATO 5A—GHANA 6A—USHER 7A—FEEDER
   1D—TIGERS 2D—MEASURE 3D—TRASHED 4D—SCORER
   Bonus: A daily occurrence—SUNSET
4. **Answers:**
   1A—CAUGHT 5A—THUMB 6A—UNTIE 7A—PLATED
   1D—CATTLE 2D—UNUSUAL 3D—HABITAT 4D—SPREAD
   Bonus: This invention dates back thousands of years—ABACUS
5. **Answers:**
   1A—NEWTON 5A—PROPS 6A—PURSE 7A—URGENT
   1D—NAPALM 2D—WHOPPER 3D—OBSERVE 4D—DECEIT
   Bonus: This place is home to nearly eight hundred thousand people—DELAWARE
6. **Answers:**
   1A—REALLY 5A—LAGER 6A—RATIO 7A—FACADE
   1D—RULING 2D—ALGERIA 3D—LORETTA 4D—BECOME
   Bonus: Type of turn—ABOUT-FACE
7. **Answers:**
   1A—HEALED 5A—LAPSE 6A—INNER 7A—STARCH
   1D—HELPER 2D—MEASURE 3D—ELEANOR 4D—SEARCH
   Bonus: Ineffective—POINTLESS
8. **Answers:**
   1A—NOVICE 5A—BASIL 6A—TEMPT 7A—ORIOLE
   1D—NABBED 2D—VISITOR 3D—COLUMBO 4D—KETTLE
   Bonus: This actor was the youngest student ever accepted into Juilliard's drama department—VAL KILMER
9. **Answers:**
   1A—ROBBER 5A—SHELL 6A—IMPEL 7A—THREAT
   1D—ROSTER 2D—BLEMISH 3D—ECLIPSE 4D—SCULPT
   Bonus: Value—CHERISH
10. **Answers:**
    1A—NEWARK 5A—MANIA 6A—LEWIS 7A—FRAYED
    1D—NUMBER 2D—WINKLER 3D—ROADWAY 4D—TOSSED
    Bonus: This man said, "Everyone is a moon, and has a dark side which he never shows to anybody."—MARK TWAIN
11. **Answers:**
    1A—REJECT 5A—COMET 6A—IRISH 7A—BASHED
    1D—RECOUP 2D—JAMAICA 3D—CATFISH 4D—LASHED
    Bonus: Repeat—DUPLICATE
12. **Answers:**
    1A—ZENITH 5A—ANITA 6A—OTHER 7A—CICADA
    1D—ZEALOT 2D—NAIROBI 3D—TRACHEA 4D—SIERRA
    Bonus: This top-rated TV show filmed 430 episodes—BONANZA
13. **Answers:**
    1A—SECOND 5A—LIMIT 6A—AMBER 7A—GENEVA
    1D—SPLASH 2D—COMPARE 3D—NOTABLE 4D—SIERRA
    Bonus: In 1913 a wooden bridge was built from the mainland to this—MIAMI BEACH
14. **Answers:**
    1A—ABACUS 5A—PILOT 6A—WAGES 7A—EDITOR
    1D—ASPECT 2D—ALLOWED 3D—UPTIGHT 4D—CURSOR
    Bonus: A type of prediction—HOROSCOPE
15. **Answers:**
    1A—BARELY 5A—VISTA 6A—OMAHA 7A—ADHERE
    1D—BOVINE 2D—RESPOND 3D—LEAKAGE 4D—ORNATE
    Bonus: The first of its kind was published in 1878—TELEPHONE BOOK
16. **Answers:**
    1A—BUFFER 5A—DINER 6A—SOGGY 7A—NEEDED
    1D—BADGER 2D—FINESSE 3D—ENRAGED 4D—SWAYED
    Bonus: The ____ ____ is 1,885 miles long—RIO GRANDE
17. **Answers:**
    1A—CASTOR 5A—BEAST 6A—GLOOM 7A—ADHERE
    1D—COBALT 2D—SNAGGED 3D—OUTDONE 4D—STYMIE
    Bonus: This word first appeared on maps in the 1500s—AMERICA
18. **Answers:**
    1A—SATIRE 5A—SCOOT 6A—BRAND 7A—JEWELS
    1D—SYSTEM 2D—TROUBLE 3D—RETRACE 4D—EXODUS
    Bonus: This place is called the "Land of Enchantment."—NEW MEXICO
19. **Answers:**
    1A—DAMNED 5A—GULCH 6A—ROBES 7A—CACTUS
    1D—DIGEST 2D—MALARIA 3D—EXHIBIT 4D—FEASTS
    Bonus: A mountain range, with peaks more than twelve thousand feet high, runs through this country from northwest to southeast—COSTA RICA
20. **Answers:**
    1A—GEMINI 5A—FACET 6A—IRONS 7A—WEAKEN
    1D—GIFTED 2D—MACHINE 3D—NETWORK 4D—LESSON
    Bonus: This U.S. state capital lies on an isthmus between lakes Monona and Mendota—MADISON
21. **Answers:**
    1A—MINCED 5A—CLUMP 6A—ROUTE 7A—SLEEVE
    1D—MOCKED 2D—NEUTRAL 3D—ESPOUSE 4D—CHEESE
    Bonus: This actor turned down the lead role in *Jerry Maguire*—TOM HANKS
22. **Answers:**
    1A—EVOLVE 5A—IDEAL 6A—STAKE 7A—GENTRY
    1D—EXITED 2D—OVERSEE 3D—VALIANT 4D—REMEDY
    Bonus: This product hit store shelves in the midtwenties—KLEENEX
23. **Answers:**
    1A—WEAPON 5A—TRACT 6A—SPIKE 7A—ADVENT
    1D—WATERY 2D—AMASSED 3D—OULINE 4D—INJECT
    Bonus: At age 10, this actor sent his résumé to *The Carol Burnett Show*—JIM CARREY
24. **Answers:**
    1A—FRIEND 5A—ABHOR 6A—MOUND 7A—INJECT
    1D—FLASHY 2D—INHUMAN 3D—NURTURE 4D—BANDIT
    Bonus: This woman said, "I'm too tall to be a girl, I never had enough dresses to be a lady, I wouldn't call myself a woman. I'd say I'm somewhere between a chick and a broad."—JULIA ROBERTS
25. **Answers:**
    1A—ORBITS 5A—ERROR 6A—ALICE 7A—FEEDER
    1D—OPENER 2D—BARGAIN 3D—TERRIER 4D—MAKEUP
    Bonus: ____, ____, is home to approximately 7 million people. It was called the "City of Kings" when it was founded in the 1500s—LIMA, PERU
26. **Answers:**
    1A—DIESEL 5A—UPPER 6A—WAGER 7A—BRIDAL
    1D—DOUBLE 2D—EMPOWER 3D—ENRAGED 4D—PATROL
    Bonus: This city, which is home to about eight hundred thousand people, was the site of the first umbrella factory in the United States—BALTIMORE
27. **Answers:**
    1A—CATCHY 5A—RUINS 6A—ELITE 7A—OTTERS
    1D—CORTEX 2D—TRIDENT 3D—HOSTILE 4D—SKIERS
    Bonus: This first U.S. ____ was authorized on March 1, 1790—CENSUS
28. **Answers:**
    1A—WOEFUL 5A—SILKY 6A—PASTA 7A—GEYSER
    1D—WISDOM 2D—ELLIPSE 3D—ULYSSES 4D—MOHAIR
    Bonus: The ____, which was not much larger than a modern tennis court, held about 100 people—MAYFLOWER
29. **Answers:**
    1A—FEDORA 5A—BASRA 6A—UTTER 7A—NEARER
    1D—FABIAN 2D—DISPUTE 3D—ROASTER 4D—BEARER
    Bonus: Until 1796, this state was called Franklin—TENNESSEE
30. **Answers:**
    1A—EXCESS 5A—WATER 6A—ZONES 7A—INVERT
    1D—EDWARD 2D—CITIZEN 3D—STRANGE 4D—CLOSET
    Bonus: The first prisoners arrived at ____ on August 11, 1934—ALCATRAZ
31. **Answers:**
    1A—GADGET 5A—MOVIE 6A—LEASE 7A—FESTER
    1D—GAMBIT 2D—DIVULGE 3D—ELEGANT 4D—METEOR
    Bonus: The first major league baseball game ever played ____ was played on April 12, 1965—INDOORS
32. **Answers:**
    1A—CAYMAN 5A—FORGE 6A—ACTOR 7A—MENDEL
    1D—COFFIN 2D—YARDAGE 3D—AVERTED 4D—PATROL
    Bonus: In 1888, this was the first European country to establish a system for health insurance for its workers—GERMANY
33. **Answers:**
    1A—MUSCLE 5A—RAVEN 6A—NOISE 7A—SHAGGY
    1D—MARLIN 2D—SEVENTH 3D—LANDING 4D—WIDELY
    Bonus: ____, ____, has more homeless cats per square mile than any other city in the world—ROME, ITALY
34. **Answers:**
    1A—DEGREE 5A—CLASS 6A—IGLOO 7A—TENNIS
    1D—DOCKET 2D—GRANITE 3D—EPSILON 4D—HERONS
    Bonus: This animal can weigh up to 300 pounds—OSTRICH

35. **Answers:**
1A—JAGUAR 5A—THING 6A—AORTA 7A—DECADE
1D—JETSON 2D—GRIMACE 3D—ALGERIA 4D—UNSAFE
Bonus: This city is home to San José Church (founded c. 1523), the oldest church in continuous use in the Western Hemisphere—SAN JUAN

36. **Answers:**
1A—ROTTEN 5A—STEER 6A—MAINE 7A—PLIGHT
1D—RUSSIA 2D—THERMAL 3D—EARNING 4D—CLIENT
Bonus: This was Mrs. Howell's seldom-talked-about first name on Gilligan's Island—EUNICE

37. **Answers:**
1A—APIECE 5A—BASIS 6A—EDICT 7A—STENCH
1D—AMBUSH 2D—INSPECT 3D—CUSHION 4D—FLETCH
Bonus: Alexander ____ was born in Nevis, British West Indies, in 1757—HAMILTON

38. **Answers:**
1A—LOCATE 5A—EXTRA 6A—HASTE 7A—CRATES
1D—LEEWAY 2D—CATCHER 3D—TRANSIT 4D—VOTERS
Bonus: This company, which is now part of a larger company, was founded in 1911—CHEVROLET

39. **Answers:**
1A—BOLTED 5A—RANGE 6A—ERNIE 7A—STORES
1D—BURIAL 2D—LENIENT 3D—ELEANOR 4D—ATHENS
Bonus: Anastasia Island, Florida, was the site of the first ____ farm in the United States, established in 1892—ALLIGATOR

40. **Answers:**
1A—STRIFE 5A—AMONG 6A—IDEAL 7A—WRITES
1D—SLACKS 2D—ROOMIER 3D—FIGMENT 4D—STYLES
Bonus: It can take 10 minutes for a ____ to fall to earth from one thousand feet—SNOWFLAKE

41. **Answers:**
1A—SAVAGE 5A—WORLD 6A—IDEAL 7A—STODGY
1D—SEWAGE 2D—VERDICT 3D—GODSEND 4D—MEDLEY
Bonus: The ringgit is the official currency of this country—MALAYSIA

42. **Answers:**
1A—RANSOM 5A—LIGHT 6A—REEVE 7A—BALLAD
1D—RELENT 2D—NIGERIA 3D—OATMEAL 4D—LEGEND
Bonus: On September 20, 1519, this man set sail with five ships and about 250 men—MAGELLAN

43. **Answers:**
1A—VACANT 5A—PRIOR 6A—ABATE 7A—HOWARD
1D—VAPORS 2D—CHICAGO 3D—NIRVANA 4D—DEFEND
Bonus: Virtually certain—IN THE BAG

44. **Answers:**
1A—LOUNGE 5A—CHINA 6A—IMPEL 7A—SEVERE
1D—LOCALE 2D—UTILIZE 3D—GRAPPLE 4D—SHELVE
Bonus: Large—COLOSSAL

45. **Answers:**
1A—REHASH 5A—CAMEL 6A—OSCAR 7A—SKUNKS
1D—RECANT 2D—HEMLOCK 3D—SILICON 4D—TWIRLS
Bonus: This show aired in the same time slot, Thursdays at 8:00 P.M. EST, during its entire nine-year run—THE WALTONS

46. **Answers:**
1A—SHRIMP 5A—UPSET 6A—FUDGE 7A—BLARES
1D—SPURNS 2D—RESTFUL 3D—MATADOR 4D—SKIERS
Bonus: Frame—SKELETON

47. **Answers:**
1A—FIGURE 5A—CLANG 6A—IRONS 7A—WEAPON
1D—FACTOR 2D—GRANITE 3D—REGROUP 4D—ALISON
Bonus: ____ ____ measures about 175 feet from top to bottom—NIAGARA FALLS

48. **Answers:**
1A—ECHOED 5A—BOGUS 6A—ALLEY 7A—PHONED
1D—EMBLEM 2D—HOGWASH 3D—EPSILON 4D—STAYED
Bonus: "The last one I had was in an airport while I was waiting to catch a flight."—SHOE SHINE

49. **Answers:**
1A—NEBULA 5A—ELLIS 6A—VOIDS 7A—GANGES
1D—NEEDLE 2D—BOLIVIA 3D—LASTING 4D—ROASTS
Bonus: Bear—TOLERATE

50. **Answers:**
1A—UNRULY 5A—HAVEN 6A—KEELS 7A—EDITED
1D—UPHILL 2D—REVOKED 3D—LENIENT 4D—MISSED
Bonus: This comedic actress said, "I always wanted to be somebody, but I should have been more specific."—LILY TOMLIN

51. **Answers:**
1A—UNWISE 5A—PILOT 6A—AMASS 7A—WEAKEN
1D—UMPIRE 2D—WALLACE 3D—SETBACK 4D—HUDSON
Bonus: "Mine usually varies each day."—BEDTIME

52. **Answers:**
1A—PUTRID 5A—PARIS 6A—ENDED 7A—STORMY
1D—POPLAR 2D—TORRENT 3D—INSIDER 4D—HEYDAY
Bonus: This country is divided into 76 provinces—THAILAND

53. **Answers:**
1A—SUBMIT 5A—TABOO 6A—LAIRS 7A—UNLESS
1D—SITTER 2D—BABYLON 3D—IDOLIZE 4D—WAISTS
Bonus: Tobacco is this country's principal cash crop—ZIMBABWE

54. **Answers:**
1A—JACKAL 5A—BRAVO 6A—RUINS 7A—ANTHEM
1D—JABBER 2D—CHAGRIN 3D—ABOLISH 4D—GYPSUM
Bonus: This country is a parliamentary democracy governed under a 1962 constitution—JAMAICA

55. **Answers:**
1A—TYRANT 5A—DIGIT 6A—MALTA 7A—INJECT
1D—TODDLE 2D—REGIMEN 3D—NATALIE 4D—DECANT
Bonus: This is up to 18 miles wide in some spots and is 27 miles long—GRAND CANYON

56. **Answers:**
1A—SLOGAN 5A—EXTRA 6A—BLANK 7A—DREAMS
1D—SLEUTH 2D—OCTOBER 3D—ALABAMA 4D—FLAKES
Bonus: This member of the rodent family loves the water—MUSKRAT

57. **Answers:**
1A—UMPIRE 5A—KHAKI 6A—ROBOT 7A—LEEWAY
1D—UNKIND 2D—PRAIRIE 3D—RAINBOW 4D—WORTHY
Bonus: This country is home to about 2.3 million people—KUWAIT

58. **Answers:**
1A—THEORY 5A—APART 6A—IDAHO 7A—UNITED
1D—TRACKS 2D—EVASION 3D—RETRACT 4D—ACCORD
Bonus: The ____ ____ lies at about 1,300 feet below sea level—DEAD SEA

59. **Answers:**
1A—JERSEY 5A—RAISE 6A—SHEET 7A—BEETLE
1D—JORDAN 2D—REISSUE 3D—ELEMENT 4D—CATTLE
Bonus: This U.S. president fathered 15 children—JOHN TYLER

60. **Answers:**
1A—CONVOY 5A—EAGLE 6A—ROAST 7A—CAVEAT
1D—CRETIN 2D—NIGERIA 3D—OPERATE 4D—SEPTET
Bonus: Donald Sutherland grew up in—NOVA SCOTIA

61. **Answers:**
1A—DEARLY 5A—WIDOW 6A—MOUSE 7A—UNITED
1D—DAWDLE 2D—ABDOMEN 3D—LAWSUIT 4D—LEGEND
Bonus: This man is pictured on a 6¢ U.S. commemorative stamp—WALT DISNEY

62. **Answers:**
1A—AMIDST 5A—TAPER 6A—SPORE 7A—PERSON
1D—ARTERY 2D—IMPASSE 3D—SERIOUS 4D—PIGEON
Bonus: These were successfully test-marketed in Cleveland, Ohio, in 1963—POP-TARTS

63. **Answers:**
1A—CANDID 5A—NOTES 6A—LEGAL 7A—NECTAR
1D—CENTER 2D—NATALIE 3D—INSIGHT 4D—DOLLAR
Bonus: Electrical ____ ____ were invented in 1892—HEARING AIDS

64. **Answers:**
1A—DOUBLE 5A—BISON 6A—REMIT 7A—TWINGE
1D—DEBRIS 2D—UNSCREW 3D—LINEMAN 4D—MYRTLE
Bonus: This man said, "I don't want to achieve immortality through my work; I want to achieve immortality through not dying."—WOODY ALLEN

65. **Answers:**
1A—PUMICE 5A—EXTRA 6A—NURSE 7A—LEANED
1D—PLEDGE 2D—MATINEE 3D—CHAGRIN 4D—SPREAD
Bonus: ____, ____, lies on the Manzanares River. It's situated on a vast, open plateau and is home to approximately 3.5 million people—MADRID, SPAIN

66. **Answers:**
1A—IMPAIR 5A—LIONS 6A—ORGAN 7A—HECTIC
1D—ISLAND 2D—PROVOKE 3D—INSIGHT 4D—PICNIC
Bonus: This man, who was born in 1899 in Brooklyn, New York, died in 1947—AL CAPONE

67. **Answers:**
1A—STREAM 5A—PRIZE 6A—SWOON 7A—CEMENT
1D—SUPPLE 2D—REISSUE 3D—AWESOME 4D—HORNET
Bonus: Oysters Rockefeller was invented in 1899 at Antoine's Restaurant in ____ ____—NEW ORLEANS

68. **Answers:**
1A—THEORY 5A—INPUT 6A—NOTES 7A—DEADLY
1D—TAILOR 2D—EXPANSE 3D—ROTATED 4D—JERSEY
Bonus: This woman was named one of *People* magazine's "50 Most Beautiful People in the World" in 1996—ASHLEY JUDD

69. **Answers:**
1A—BALBOA 5A—CANDY 6A—EXPEL 7A—EDISON
1D—BUCKET 2D—LINSEED 3D—OLYMPUS 4D—MERLIN
Bonus: Steven Spielberg was offered a chance to direct this film, but the producers balked at his salary demands—SUPERMAN

70. **Answers:**
1A—YEARLY 5A—LEMON 6A—NAMES 7A—SCENES
1D—YELLED 2D—ALMANAC 3D—LINEMAN 4D—NOISES
Bonus: The ancient ____ made knives from volcanic glass—MAYANS

71. **Answers:**
1A—JOSEPH 5A—ACORN 6A—KOALA 7A—GRITTY
1D—JOANNA 2D—SHOCKER 3D—PENDANT 4D—INFAMY
Bonus: On his fourth voyage to the Americas, Columbus was marooned on ____ for more than a year—JAMAICA

72. **Answers:**
1A—UNKIND 5A—PILOT 6A—ALICE 7A—LEAGUE
1D—UMPIRE 2D—KILDARE 3D—NOTHING 4D—FLEECE
Bonus: ____ Center consists of 19 buildings situated on 22 acres—ROCKEFELLER

73. **Answers:**
1A—COMMON 5A—SOLVE 6A—RADON 7A—WATERY
1D—CASINO 2D—MALARIA 3D—OVERDUE 4D—MAINLY
Bonus: Much of ____, ____, was destroyed by fire in 1624—OSLO, NORWAY

74. **Answers:**
1A—AUSTIN 5A—GUEST 6A—KENYA 7A—ORDEAL
1D—ANGLED 2D—SPEAKER 3D—INTENSE 4D—BEFALL
Bonus: The nest of a ____ ____ can weigh up to one ton—BALD EAGLE

75. **Answers:**
1A—CLAUSE 5A—RACER 6A—EXTRA 7A—ETCHED
1D—CORBIN 2D—ANCIENT 3D—SCRATCH 4D—DEMAND
Bonus: The United States launched its first ____ ____ in January 1954—ATOMIC SUB

76. **Answers:**
1A—ALPACA 5A—MONET 6A—CHASE 7A—LATELY
1D—ARMADA 2D—PANACEA 3D—COTTAGE 4D—NICELY
Bonus: The ____ were canceled in 1916, 1940, and 1944—OLYMPICS

77. **Answers:**
1A—SPOKEN 5A—RATES 6A—EXACT 7A—SLEEPS
1D—STRAND 2D—OATMEAL 3D—ENSNARE 4D—WRITES
Bonus: This former professional soccer player was inducted into the Rock and Roll Hall of Fame in 1994—ROD STEWART

78. **Answers:**
1A—MICRON 5A—UNIFY 6A—PAPER 7A—SEASON
1D—MAULED 2D—CRIPPLE 3D—OLYMPUS 4D—PATRON
Bonus: ____ is about the same size as Maine—SCOTLAND

79. **Answers:**
1A—COERCE 5A—PLATO 6A—ASKED 7A—GENDER
1D—COPIES 2D—EMANATE 3D—CLOAKED 4D—GLIDER
Bonus: The ____ Islands were discovered in 1535 by the Spanish navigator Tomás Berlanga—GALÁPAGOS

80. **Answers:**
1A—VIOLET 5A—WASTE 6A—UNTIL 7A—GENRES
1D—VOWELS 2D—OBSCURE 3D—ERECTOR 4D—SHELLS
Bonus: This "rock collection" dates back thousands of years—STONEHENGE

81. **Answers:**
1A—TREATY 5A—ORGAN 6A—INSET 7A—SHEARS
1D—TROWEL 2D—ENGLISH 3D—TUNISIA 4D—GRATIS
Bonus: On average, this kills about 73 people annually in the United States—LIGHTNING

82. **Answers:**
1A—COUPLE 5A—LAURA 6A—UNION 7A—BLIGHT
1D—CALLED 2D—UNUSUAL 3D—LEANING 4D—MAGNET
Bonus: The ____ alphabet has more than 70 letters—CAMBODIAN

83. **Answers:**
1A—HITCHED 5A—UNCAP 6A—INEPT 7A—INGESTS
1D—HOUDINI 2D—TACKING 3D—HAPLESS 4D—DONATES
Bonus: There are about nine hundred thousand species of these—INSECTS

84. **Answers:**
1A—FIFTEEN 5A—COILS 6A—TELLS 7A—SHRINKS
1D—FACTORS 2D—FRITTER 3D—EPSILON 4D—NUDISTS
Bonus: Finding words that rhyme with *month* and *orange*, for example—DIFFICULT

85. **Answers:**
1A—SCHEME 5A—HOMER 6A—TWINE 7A—GRADES
1D—SCHOOL 2D—HAMSTER 3D—MARRIED 4D—ALIENS
Bonus: This TV show was rated number two four times but never reached the top spot—ROSEANNE

86. **Answers:**
1A—LIBERAL 5A—ATLAS 6A—OCTET 7A—SENIORS
1D—LOATHES 2D—BALLOON 3D—RISOTTO 4D—LOCATES
Bonus: This city was almost completely destroyed by an earthquake in 1755—CASABLANCA

87. **Answers:**
1A—MALARIA 5A—STUNG 6A—DIMES 7A—SHRINES
1D—MISFITS 2D—LAUNDER 3D—REGIMEN 4D—ADJUSTS
Bonus: This takes up about 23 square miles—MANHATTAN

88. **Answers:**
1A—DIREFUL 5A—MOTTO 6A—TRADE 7A—SADNESS
1D—DAMAGES 2D—ROTATED 3D—FOOTAGE 4D—LAWLESS
Bonus: In 1975 this actor graduated from Western Michigan University with a degree in television production—TIM ALLEN

89. **Answers:**
1A—CRACKER 5A—LEMON 6A—NEPAL 7A—SPANNED
1D—CELTICS 2D—AMMONIA 3D—KINGPIN 4D—RUFFLED
Bonus: This person, who died in 1945, said, "I keep my ideals, because in spite of everything, I still believe that people are really good at heart."—ANNE FRANK

90. **Answers:**
1A—AFFIRM 5A—LATIN 6A—FRILL 7A—FLIGHT
1D—ABLAZE 2D—FATEFUL 3D—RANTING 4D—PIGLET
Bonus: Begin—INITIATE

91. **Answers:**
1A—LAWFUL 5A—SWARM 6A—PIVOT 7A—CREDIT
1D—LASTLY 2D—WRAPPER 3D—UNMOVED 4D—SEPTET
Bonus: This woman said, "It's not the men in your life that count, it's the life in your men."—MAE WEST

92. **Answers:**
1A—PIGSTY 5A—KENYA 6A—INPUT 7A—NEARBY
1D—PEKING 2D—GENUINE 3D—TRAPPER 4D—SOFTLY
Bonus: This country is about the same size as Indiana (approximately thirty-five thousand square miles)—PORTUGAL

93. **Answers:**
1A—PETITE 5A—CHILL 6A—THING 7A—BRIDGE
1D—PICKLE 2D—TWISTER 3D—TALLIED 4D—GAGGLE
Bonus: This U.S. state capital is home to about two hundred thousand people—RALEIGH

94. **Answers:**
1A—CATCHY 5A—ANNOY 6A—RAISE 7A—IMPEND
1D—CRAYON 2D—TANTRUM 3D—HAYWIRE 4D—FRIEND
Bonus: This country is larger than Texas but smaller than Alaska—SOUTH AFRICA

95. **Answers:**
1A—MADCAP 5A—MOVIE 6A—LEAPT 7A—HERESY
1D—MOMENT 2D—DIVULGE 3D—AVERAGE 4D—WORTHY
Bonus: The first coin-operated vending machines in the United States dispensed this—CHEWING GUM

96. **Answers:**
1A—AGATHA 5A—ROOMS 6A—IGLOO 7A—SHORES
1D—AFRAID 2D—ABOLISH 3D—HUSTLER 4D—BROOKS
Bonus: These are found all along United States highways—BILLBOARDS

97. **Answers:**
1A—PAGODA 5A—FIRST 6A—FLAIR 7A—HEATER
1D—PUFFIN 2D—GIRAFFE 3D—DETRACT 4D—NEARER
Bonus: The ____ is made up of 12 provinces—NETHERLANDS

98. **Answers:**
1A—DIAPER 5A—RATED 6A—CARDS 7A—JEWELS
1D—DURESS 2D—ATTACHÉ 3D—ENDORSE 4D—KANSAS
Bonus: Nosocomephobia is the fear of ____—HOSPITALS

99. **Answers:**
1A—DIESEL 5A—ROUTE 6A—AZTEC 7A—FENDER
1D—DARWIN 2D—EDUCATE 3D—ELECTED 4D—CONCUR
Bonus: No settlement in this country is more than 75 miles from the sea—NEW ZEALAND

100. **Answers:**
1A—RECITE 5A—SATIN 6A—DOGMA 7A—ELATED
1D—RESORT 2D—CITADEL 3D—TONIGHT 4D—POLAND
Bonus: This man was a prizefighter, steel mill laborer, and gas station attendant before seeing his first glimmer of fame—DEAN MARTIN

101. **Answers:**
1A—TRAFFIC 5A—GECKO 6A—HAITI 7A—RELEASE
1D—TIGHTER 2D—ALCOHOL 3D—FLORIDA 4D—CYANIDE
Bonus: This U.S. president was born in Ohio—GARFIELD

102. **Answers:**
1A—DEVOTED 5A—OMEGA 6A—NOTES 7A—REMARKS
1D—DROPPER 2D—VIETNAM 3D—TRACTOR 4D—DETESTS
Bonus: The American ____ ____ was organized in 1881—RED CROSS

103. **Answers:**
1A—BISECT 5A—ORION 6A—REEDS 7A—APATHY
1D—BROOKS 2D—STIRRUP 3D—CONNECT 4D—PIGSTY
Bonus: ____ ____ were introduced in 1929—RICE KRISPIES

104. **Answers:**
1A—SNAPPY 5A—RAISE 6A—OZARK 7A—FAULTY
1D—STROBE 2D—ARIZONA 3D—PREVAIL 4D—MEEKLY
Bonus: This automobile pioneer lived from 1844 to 1929—KARL BENZ

105. **Answers:**
1A—FREELY 5A—WORMS 6A—GLOAT 7A—EDISON
1D—FEWEST 2D—ENRAGED 3D—LASSOES 4D—PROTON
Bonus: This woman said, "I'm not offended by dumb blonde jokes because I know that I'm not dumb. I also know I'm not blonde—DOLLY PARTON

106. **Answers:**
1A—PAGODA 5A—RAZOR 6A—LIBRA 7A—DECEIT
1D—PARODY 2D—GAZELLE 3D—DURABLE 4D—RECANT
Bonus: ____, ____, is home to about 7 million people. It was founded in 969. Tourism is important to its economy—CAIRO, EGYPT

107. **Answers:**
1A—ICEMAN 5A—THEME 6A—GLOVE 7A—ADVENT
1D—INTAKE 2D—EMERGED 3D—AWESOME 4D—ATTEST
Bonus: At one point most homes in the United States had one, but now fewer than 50 percent do—TV ANTENNA

108. **Answers:**
1A—THEMES 5A—SABLE 6A—ERODE 7A—USHERS
1D—TISSUE 2D—EMBLEMS 3D—EYESORE 4D—AGREES
Bonus: The U.S.____ Service was founded on August 7, 1789—LIGHTHOUSE

109. **Answers:**
1A—APPEAR 5A—CHOKE 6A—ACORN 7A—REMEDY
1D—ASCEND 2D—PROBATE 3D—AWESOME 4D—MAINLY
Bonus: The first ____ ____ was issued by the U.S. government in 1862—PAPER MONEY

110. **Answers:**
1A—JUMPER 5A—COCOA 6A—EDITS 7A—THREAT
1D—JACKET 2D—MACBETH 3D—EXAMINE 4D—BASSET
Bonus: In 1951 ____ ____ ____ ____ opened its first restaurant in San Diego, California, pioneering the drive-through concept and featuring 18¢ hamburgers—JACK IN THE BOX

111. **Answers:**
1A—PROMPT 5A—UNTIL 6A—ASCOT 7A—SKATER
1D—PLUCKY 2D—OUTBACK 3D—POLECAT 4D—GUITAR
Bonus: In 1400 B.C., it was the fashion among rich ____ women to place a large cone of scented grease on top of their heads—EGYPTIAN

112. **Answers:**
1A—ACCEPT 5A—PLUTO 6A—AMEND 7A—JERSEY
1D—APPLES 2D—CRUSADE 3D—PROFESS 4D—KINDLY
Bonus: On June 22, 1870, the U.S. Congress created the Department of ____—JUSTICE

113. **Answers:**
1A—OSPREY 5A—CLEFT 6A—ENACT 7A—STATED
1D—ORCHID 2D—PRESENT 3D—EXTRACT 4D—LASTED
Bonus: ____, ____, was founded in the mid-1800s. Many of the new settlers were French immigrants from the failed colony La Reunion—DALLAS, TEXAS

114. **Answers:**
1A—BOULDER 5A—SKIDS 6A—OMEGA 7A—DONATED
1D—BUSTLED 2D—UNICORN 3D—DISSECT 4D—RICHARD
Bonus: There are about 32 species of these, and all of them are venomous—SEA SNAKES

115. **Answers:**
1A—PHONICS 5A—GATES 6A—MEALS 7A—SENATOR
1D—PIGLETS 2D—OTTOMAN 3D—INSTANT 4D—SPONSOR
Bonus: Mischievous activities—SHENANIGANS

116. **Answers:**
1A—RAGTIME 5A—CLOUD 6A—PIANO 7A—SURPASS
1D—RECOUPS 2D—GROUPER 3D—INDIANA 4D—EDITORS
Bonus: ____ has the world's highest number of livestock per person—MONGOLIA

117. **Answers:**
1A—PAPOOSE 5A—ORBIT 6A—LACES 7A—MUSCLED
1D—PROGRAM 2D—PEBBLES 3D—OPTICAL 4D—ELAPSED
Bonus: This word's origin dates back to about the second century—ABRACADABRA

118. **Answers:**
1A—SINKING 5A—UNTIE 6A—CRAWL 7A—RESIDES
1D—SLUMBER 2D—NOTICES 3D—ICELAND 4D—GARBLES
Bonus: This actor turned down the males lead in *Ghost*—BRUCE WILLIS

119. **Answers:**
1A—SHOPPER 5A—OCEAN 6A—DRUGS 7A—ETERNAL
1D—SCOURGE 2D—OVERDUE 3D—PENGUIN 4D—REFUSAL
Bonus: As a way of honoring his work with the environment, this actor was asked to name a new breed of butterfly. He named it after his daughter, Georgia—HARRISON FORD

120. **Answers:**
1A—TANTRUM 5A—CREAM 6A—LLAMA 7A—SYSTEMS
1D—TICKETS 2D—NEEDLES 3D—RAMPAGE 4D—MONDAYS
Bonus: This member of the Rock and Roll Hall of Fame was born in Newark, New Jersey, on October 13, 1941—PAUL SIMON

121. **Answers:**
1A—BLOUSE 5A—COTTA 6A—OOMPH 7A—WEDDED
1D—BECKON 2D—OUTCOME 3D—SWARMED 4D—RUSHED
Bonus: The Environmental Protection Agency estimated that gas—powered ____ ____ contribute to about 5 percent of ozone pollution in the United States—LAWN MOWERS

122. **Answers:**
1A—TOPSOIL 5A—SHEEP 6A—GREAT 7A—RESISTS
1D—TASTIER 2D—PLEDGES 3D—OPPRESS 4D—LENGTHS
Bonus: This is one of the largest ports in the world and home to more than 16 millions people—SHANGHAI

123. **Answers:**
1A—PACKAGE 5A—TRACK 6A—LLAMA 7A—RESIDUE
1D—PITCHER 2D—CHABLIS 3D—AWKWARD 4D—ENSNARE
Bonus: You have millions of these in your body—SWEAT GLANDS

124. **Answers:**
1A—SPENDER 5A—GLUES 6A—INANE 7A—SLEUTHS
1D—SIGNALS 2D—ELUSIVE 3D—DISTANT 4D—RENDERS
Bonus: This country is about the same size as South Dakota (about seventy-five thousand square miles)—SENEGAL

125. **Answers:**
1A—APRICOT 5A—ROOMY 6A—IRENE 7A—PEGASUS
1D—AIRSHIP 2D—ROOTING 3D—COYNESS 4D—TICKETS
Bonus: "I feel that today's puzzle is harder than yesterday's."—COMPARISON

126. **Answers:**
1A—WARSAW 5A—CAVES 6A—RURAL 7A—GERALD
1D—WICKED 2D—REVERSE 3D—AUSTRIA 4D—BALLAD
Bonus: This puzzle's hints, for example—VAGUE CLUES

127. **Answers:**
1A—SETTLED 5A—ADAPT 6A—HAITI 7A—SLAMMED
1D—STATUES 2D—TRACHEA 3D—LITHIUM 4D—DIRTIED
Bonus: This runs from east to west about 2,400 miles and from north to south about 2,000 miles—AUSTRALIA

128. **Answers:**
1A—SERPENT 5A—LOCKS 6A—THETA 7A—TALENTS
1D—SOLICIT 2D—RECITAL 3D—EASTERN 4D—TARMACS
Bonus: More than 400 young men tried out for the lead roles on this sitcom—THE MONKEES

129. **Answers:**
1A—REBIRTH 5A—HARDY 6A—LOOPS 7A—STRIDES
1D—REHIRES 2D—BURGLAR 3D—RAYMOND 4D—HEARSES
Bonus: There are currently three of these in operation and based in three different regions of the United States—GOODYEAR BLIMPS

130. **Answers:**
1A—STANZAS 5A—*NORMA* 6A—AGAIN 7A—MATADOR
1D—SANCTUM 2D—ABREAST 3D—ZEALAND 4D—SEMINAR
Bonus: There are just four of these in the 48 contiguous United States—TIME ZONES

131. **Answers:**
1A—COMICAL 5A—RATES 6A—VEILS 7A—RESENTS
1D—CARRIER 2D—MOTIVES 3D—CASPIAN 4D—LOCUSTS
Bonus: End—TERMINATE

132. **Answers:**
1A—RESTIVE 5A—CHAOS 6A—INERT 7A—RELATED
1D—RECOVER 2D—SPANIEL 3D—INSPECT 4D—EMITTED
Bonus: This woman said, "I know God will not give me anything I can't handle. I just wish that he didn't trust me so much."—MOTHER TERESA

133. **Answers:**
1A—DECIMAL 5A—BASIN 6A—IMAGE 7A—SUNDAES
1D—DEBATES 2D—CASPIAN 3D—MONTANA 4D—LINGERS
Bonus: The ____ ____ was established in 1945—UNITED NATIONS

134. **Answers:**
1A—UNWRAP 5A—SLANG 6A—GLIDE 7A—METHOD
1D—UNSAFE 2D—WRANGLE 3D—ANGUISH 4D—ASCEND
Bonus: This cartoon figure debuted in 1852—UNCLE SAM

135. **Answers:**
1A—PERSON 5A—RIVET 6A—SIREN 7A—ADJOIN
1D—PHRASE 2D—REVISED 3D—ONTARIO 4D—CANNON
Bonus: A deltiologist collects these—POSTCARDS

136. **Answers:**
1A—DAWNED 5A—RHINE 6A—TROOP 7A—SECEDE
1D—DURESS 2D—WHISTLE 3D—EYESORE 4D—SIMPLE
Bonus: This state is home to more than 8,500 lakes—WISCONSIN

137. **Answers:**
1A—NABBED 5A—SWAMP 6A—DINER 7A—ORDEAL
1D—NASSAU 2D—BLADDER 3D—EXPANSE 4D—PLURAL
Bonus: McDonald's and Burger King—PROPER NAMES

138. **Answers:**
1A—JUMBLED 5A—SATIN 6A—DRONE 7A—SHRINKS
1D—JESTERS 2D—MATADOR 3D—LINCOLN 4D—DECREES
Bonus: This U.S. politician was born in 1936, in the Panama Canal Zone—JOHN McCAIN

139. **Answers:**
1A—JAMMED 5A—DONOR 6A—REALM 7A—SNAKES
1D—JUDGED 2D—MONARCH 3D—EARMARK 4D—CLIMBS
Bonus: Some people are surprised to learn that this actor never won an Emmy—JACKIE GLEASON

140. **Answers:**
1A—NUCLEUS 5A—SEIZE 6A—KOALA 7A—SINCERE
1D—NESTLES 2D—CHICKEN 3D—ELEVATE 4D—STORAGE
Bonus: There are more than 60 million ____ ____ books in print—STAR TREK

141. **Answers:**
1A—JAILED 5A—ABHOR 6A—BATES 7A—EDICTS
1D—JOANNA 2D—ICHABOD 3D—ERRATIC 4D—WHISKS
Bonus: This actor, whose middle name is Joseph, was born on April 22, 1937, in New Jersey—JACK NICHOLSON

142. **Answers:**
1A—JOHNSON 5A—COMMA 6A—TRIPE 7A—SCRAGGY
1D—JOCKEYS 2D—HAMSTER 3D—STAYING 4D—NURSERY
Bonus: This actor's first job as an entertainer was as a female dancer in a chorus line—JAMES CAGNEY

143. **Answers:**
1A—UPPITY 5A—ACORN 6A—EAGER 7A—BRUTAL
1D—URANUS 2D—PIONEER 3D—TONIGHT 4D—BARREL
Bonus: ____ debuted on store shelves in 1941—CHEERIOS

144. **Answers:**
1A—LETHAL 5A—GUEST 6A—INCAS 7A—AGREED
1D—LEGUME 2D—TEEMING 3D—ATTACHÉ 4D—UNUSED
Bonus: This actress is the only actress to win a Golden Globe, an Oscar®, and an Emmy in the same calendar year (as of 2004)—HELEN HUNT

145. **Answers:**
1A—MATURE 5A—VAULT 6A—TWINE 7A—RECKON
1D—MOVING 2D—TRUSTEE 3D—RETHINK 4D—CAVERN
Bonus: This man said, "I was trained to be an actor, not a star. I was trained to play roles, not to deal with fame and agents and lawyers and the press."—GENE HACKMAN

146. **Answers:**
1A—ASSETS 5A—SPACE 6A—GORGE 7A—TRUMAN
1D—ASSIGN 2D—SWAGGER 3D—THEOREM 4D—SCREEN
Bonus: ____, ____, is home to approximately 3 million people. It was conquered in the 1450s by the Ottoman Turks, who held it for almost four centuries—ATHENS, GREECE

147. **Answers:**
1A—DIETED 5A—STEEP 6A—OMAHA 7A—PEANUT
1D—DISMAY 2D—EYESORE 3D—EXPLAIN 4D—MUTANT
Bonus: Scholars believe that this nursery rhyme is more than 500 years old—HUMPTY DUMPTY

148. **Answers:**
1A—SKEWER 5A—AMPLE 6A—SLEEK 7A—EDITOR
1D—SPARED 2D—EXPOSED 3D—ELEMENT 4D—BACKER
Bonus: This man was the only network anchor present at the collapse of the Berlin Wall in 1989—TOM BROKAW

149. **Answers:**
1A—METEOR 5A—BLUES 6A—FORCE 7A—REPEAT
1D—MOBBED 2D—TRUFFLE 3D—OBSERVE 4D—CAVEAT
Bonus: ____ rank as one of the safest forms of transportation, with only one fatality every 100 million miles traveled—ELEVATORS

150. **Answers:**
1A—DEPICT 5A—RAYON 6A—ERROR 7A—STOLEN
1D—DIRECT 2D—PAYMENT 3D—CONTROL 4D—MICRON
Bonus: The first known ____ date back to ancient Greece—ENCYCLOPEDIAS

151. **Answers:**
1A—SCREWY 5A—NOBEL 6A—RACES 7A—RHYTHM
1D—SANELY 2D—REBIRTH 3D—WILDCAT 4D—BALSAM
Bonus: Construction on the ____ ____ began in 1961—BERLIN WALL

152. **Answers:**
1A—BEHOLD 5A—ROTOR 6A—FREUD 7A—PLATES
1D—BARIUM 2D—HATEFUL 3D—LARGEST 4D—PANDAS
Bonus: As recently as the thirties, ____ injections were commonly used by physicians to treat alcoholism—MORPHINE

153. **Answers:**
1A—SHRILL 5A—MOWED 6A—IRISH 7A—LENGTH
1D—SUMMIT 2D—RAWHIDE 3D—LODGING 4D—EIGHTH
Bonus: The ____ and its landscaped grounds occupy 18 acres of ground—WHITE HOUSE

154. **Answers:**
1A—JACKAL 5A—RANGE 6A—SCOWL 7A—MAKEUP
1D—JERSEY 2D—CANASTA 3D—AWESOME 4D—WALLOP
Bonus: ____, ____, lies on the Kanto plain. It's intersected by the Sumida River and has an extensive network of canals—TOKYO, JAPAN

155. **Answers:**
1A—BIGGEST 5A—LEEKS 6A—FENCE 7A—RELIEVE
1D—BOLSTER 2D—GLEEFUL 3D—ESSENCE 4D—TRAPEZE
Bonus: Approximately 95 percent of all the Earth's animal species are ____—INVERTEBRATES

156. **Answers:**
1A—SLEEPER 5A—CLEAN 6A—ANITA 7A—SKEWERS
1D—SECTORS 2D—ELEVATE 3D—PENSIVE 4D—REDCAPS
Bonus: In the United States, the standard width between ____ ____ is 4 feet, 8½ inches—RAILROAD TRACKS

157. **Answers:**
1A—MAGICAL 5A—GROOM 6A—GRIPE 7A—SKATERS
1D—MAGNETS 2D—GEORGIA 3D—COMPILE 4D—LISTENS
Bonus: This movie won Oscars® for Best Picture, Best Actor, Best Director, and Best Original Screenplay—*RAIN MAN*

158. **Answers:**
1A—CAPITAL 5A—HOUND 6A—BRENT 7A—STRATUS
1D—COHORTS 2D—PLUMBER 3D—TIDIEST 4D—LOCATES
Bonus: The average adult ____ ____ weighs from 2.25 pounds to 3.25 pounds—HUMAN BRAIN

159. **Answers:**
1A—WITHERS 5A—APART 6A—FLUTE 7A—EXCITES
1D—WRANGLE 2D—TRAFFIC 3D—ENTRUST 4D—SUBLETS
Bonus: Certain—INFALLIBLE

160. **Answers:**
1A—HOSIERY 5A—STAMP 6A—EXUDE 7A—ENDLESS
1D—HOSPICE 2D—SEAWEED 3D—ESPOUSE 4D—YANKEES
Bonus: ____ ____ service began in 1860—PONY EXPRESS

161. **Answers:**
1A—PAROLE 5A—ACCUSAL 6A—CHEMIST 7A—STAGES
1D—PRANCE 2D—RICHEST 3D—LASTING 4D—SLATES
Double Bonus: Protects—INSURES
Type of ending and beginning—SUNRISE

162. **Answers:**
1A—SOLEMN 5A—INCENSE 6A—CONSOLE 7A—REPELS
1D—SWITCH 2D—LICENSE 3D—MANHOLE 4D—METERS
Double Bonus: Automotive pioneer Ferdinand ____—PORSCHE
Attached structures—PORCHES

163. **Answers:**
1A—UPBEAT 5A—SHINGLE 6A—RETREAD 7A—ALISON
1D—UNSURE 2D—BRISTOL 3D—ALGIERS 4D—TENDON
Double Bonus: ____ loan—STUDENT
Underdeveloped—STUNTED

164. **Answers:**
1A—COMBAT 5A—RALEIGH 6A—SEAPORT 7A—SEDANS
1D—CORPSE 2D—MILEAGE 3D—ARIZONA 4D—PHOTOS
Double Bonus: Driving ____—DIRECTIONS
Prudence—DISCRETION

165. **Answers:**
1A—LAUREL 5A—TREASON 6A—SURPLUS 7A—PHONED
1D—LATEST 2D—UNEARTH 3D—EPSILON 4D—UNUSE
Double Bonus: 1986 movie—ALIENS
____ solution—SALINE

166. **Answers:**
1A—ANGLED 5A—UNUSUAL 6A—NOMADIC 7A—STORED
1D—ALUMNI 2D—GOURMET 3D—ECUADOR 4D—SLICED
Double Bonus: Warmer—MILDER
Singer-actress born in New Jersey—MIDLER

167. **Answers:**
1A—RAFFLE 5A—BOOSTER 6A—LARGEST 7A—EDISON
1D—RUBBLE 2D—FLOORED 3D—LETTERS 4D—PROTON
Double Bonus: Position—BEARINGS
Intrudes—BARGES IN

168. **Answers:**
1A—CHILLY 5A—INSPIRE 6A—EXECUTE 7A—STREAM
1D—COILED 2D—INSPECT 3D—LEISURE 4D—REDEEM
Double Bonus: Inconvenient—UNTIMELY
Insignificant—MINUTELY

169. **Answers:**
1A—DEDUCE 5A—AUSTRIA 6A—EPISODE 7A—SEASON
1D—DEALER 2D—DESPISE 3D—CURIOUS 4D—CAVERN
Double Bonus: Released—PAROLED
Snow ____ or ____ moth—LEOPARD

170. **Answers:**
1A—REVIEW 5A—SERPENT 6A—EXITING 7A—DODGES
1D—RUSHED 2D—VERTIGO 3D—EVENING 4D—STAGES
Double Bonus: Harsh—SEVERE
Actor born in 1964—REEVES

171. **Answers:**
1A—DISMAL 5A—TWINE 6A—DROLL 7A—REVERT
1D—DATING 2D—SWINDLE 3D—AWESOME 4D—EYELET
Double Bonus: Angrily—IRATELY
____ check—REALITY

172. **Answers:**
1A—HIATUS 5A—CHEDDAR 6A—EXAMINE 7A—MERGES
1D—HACKED 2D—AVERAGE 3D—UNDYING 4D—GREENS
Double Bonus: A mythical female—MEDUSA
Entertained—AMUSED

173. **Answers:**
1A—ISSUED 5A—OPINE 6A—DEGAS 7A—TENDON
1D—IRONIC 2D—SWINDLE 3D—EMERGED 4D—CHOSEN
Double Bonus: Together—UNITED
Not fastened—UNTIED

174. **Answers:**
1A—MANNER 5A—STUNTED 6A—SPINNER 7A—CHUTES
1D—MISUSE 2D—NOURISH 3D—EXTINCT 4D—ADORNS
Triple Bonus: A tennis player's first name—MARTINA
Type of alien—MARTIAN
Type of monkey—TAMARIN

175. **Answers:**
1A—CORPSE 5A—RAMBLED 6A—ADAMANT 7A—ATTEND
1D—CORRAL 2D—REMNANT 3D—SALVAGE 4D—EDITED
Triple Bonus: Birthday ____—PARTIES
Thieves—PIRATES
Type of walk—TRAIPSE

176. **Answers:**
1A—SIENNA 5A—AVERTED 6A—CLEARER 7A—STALLS
1D—SEARCH 2D—ELEMENT 3D—NATURAL 4D—ADORES
Triple Bonus: Re-educate—RETRAIN
A piece of land—TERRAIN
Type of instructor—TRAINER

177. **Answers:**
1A—SLATED 5A—SNAKE 6A—ICTUS 7A—ENERGY
1D—SYSTEM 2D—ARABIAN 3D—ERECTOR 4D—GLOSSY
Triple Bonus: Early road builders—ROMANS
Lordly dwellings—MANORS
1996 M.G. movie—RANSOM

178. **Answers:**
1A—LATENT 5A—MIMIC 6A—UPSET 7A—CABANA
1D—LIMBER 2D—TEMPURA 3D—NICOSIA 4D—AGATHA
Triple Bonus: Important building—CAPITOL
____ fiber or disk—OPTICAL
Of local interest—TOPICAL